Contents

Introduction

This wordlist gives you a comprehensive – if not exhaustive – list of common words. The appendices provide you with further groups of words which have more specific applications. You will see that you should be able to write any word not included by using the outline of a similar word as a guide and applying Teeline principles to the longhand.

As the language changes and develops, special forms come in and out of common usage. In this new edition, we have included the special forms which appear in all of our Teeline books. They are presented in bold type.

The flexibility of Teeline means that there may be alternative – and equally correct – outlines for a word.

Where there are alternative outlines, either both are shown, or the one chosen is that which is considered to be the easiest or quickest to write. For instance, PROFESSIONAL can be written either

.... or ....

The former outline keeps more strictly to Teeline theory, but the latter avoids splitting the outline into three separate sections, thus reducing writing time.

The writer's own preferred outline may be added if this differs from the one given.

Special contraction of words

Where words are contracted for use in groupings or as word beginnings or endings, this is shown in brackets, as follows:

(g) — in groupings,
(b) — as a word beginning,
(e) — as a word ending.

Examples of these are:

Hundred, which is.............. standing alone, but.............. when used in groupings.

Super, which is .... standing alone, but .... when used as a word beginning, and
Word, which is .... standing alone, but .... when used as a word ending or in groupings.

Teeline GOLD

Word List

This edition compiled by Mavis Smith and Anne Tilly

HEINEMANN EDUCATIONAL

Heinemann Educational,
a division of Heinemann Educational Books Ltd,
Halley Court, Jordan Hill, Oxford OX2 8EJ

OXFORD LONDON EDINBURGH
MADRID ATHENS BOLOGNA PARIS
MELBOURNE SYDNEY AUCKLAND SINGAPORE
TOKYO IBADAN NAIROBI HARARE
GABORONE PORTSMOUTH NH (USA)

First published 1981. This edition published 1992.

93 94 95 96 97 11 10 9 8 7 6 5 4 3 2

A catalogue record is available from the British Library on request.
ISBN 0 435 45359 9

Designed by Gecko Limited, Bicester, Oxon
Printed in England
by Clays Ltd, St Ives plc

Other Teeline titles available
Teeline Gold: **The Course Book** edited by Meriel Bowers
Teeline Gold: **Workbook** by Harry Butler
Teeline Gold: **Speed Ladder** by Meriel Bowers and Stephanie Hall
Teeline Word Groupings by George Hill
New Teeline Dictation Book edited by George Hill
Teeline Shorthand Dictation Passages by Dorothy Bowyer
Handbook for Teeline Teachers edited by Harry Butler
Medical Teeline by Pat Garner and Pat Clare

abandon

abate/ment

abbey

abbreviate

abbreviation

abdicate

abdomen

abduct

abhor/rent

abide

abiding

ability (e)

abject

ablaze

able (e)

ably (e)

abnormal or

abnormality or

aboard

abode

abolish

abolition

abominable

abort/ion

abortive

abound

about

about-turn

above (b)

above-board

abrasive

abreast

abridge/ment

abroad

abrupt

abscond

abseil

absence or

absent or

absentee or

absenteeism or

absolute

absolutely or

absorb/ent

abstain

abstainer

abstention

abstract

abstruse

absurd

abundance

abundant/ly

abuse/d

abusive

academic

academy ....

ACAS ....

accede ....

accelerate .... or ....

acceleration .... or ....

accelerator .... or ....

accent ....

accentual ....

accentuate ....

accept/able ....

acceptance ....

access/ible ....

accessories ....

accident/al .... or ....

acclaim ....

acclamation ....

acclimatisation ....

acclimatise ....

accolade ....

accommodate .... or ....

accommodation .... or ....

accompaniment ....

accompany ....

accomplice ....

accomplish/ment ....

accordance .... or ....

according/ly .... or ....

accost/ed ....

account/s ....

accountable .... or ....

accountancy .... or ....

accountant .... or ....

accredit ....

accrue ....

accumulate ....

accuracy ....

accurate/ly ....

accusal ....

accusation ....

accuse/d ....

accustom/ed ....

ace ....

acerbic ....

acetate ....

acetone ....

ache ....

achieve/ment ....

acid ....

acidic ....

acidity ....

acknowledge .... or ....

acknowledgement .... or ....

acoustics ....

acquaint/ance ....

acquiesce/nce ....

acquire/d ....

acquisition ....

acquital ....

acre/age ....

acrimony ....

acrobat/ics ....

acronym .... or ....

across ....

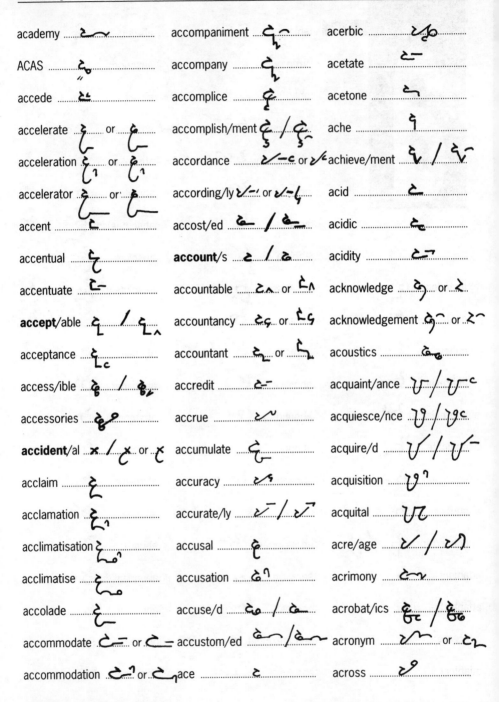

acrylic ... or ...
act ...
action ...
activate ...
active ...
activist ...
activity ... or ...
actor ...
actress/es ...
actual ...
actuality ... or ...
actuary ...
actuate ...
acumen ...
acupuncture ... or ...
acute/ly ...
adage ...
adamant ...
adapt/able ...
adaptation ...
adapter/or ...

adaptive ...
add/ed ...
addend ...
addendum ...
addict ...
addition/al ...
additives ...
address ...
adept ...
adequate/ly ...
adhere/nce ...
adherent ...
adhesive ...
ad hoc ...
ad infinitum ... or ...
adjacent ...
adjoin ...
adjourn ...
adjudicate ...
adjudicator ...
adjust/ment ...

ad lib ...
administer ... or ...
administrate ... or ...
administration ... or ...
administrator ... or ...
admirable ...
admire ...
admirer ...
admissible ...
admission ...
admit ...
admittance ...
admitted ...
admittedly ...
admonish ...
ad nauseam ...
adolescence ...
adolescent ...
adopt ...
adoptive ...
adorable ...

adorably
adoration
adore
adrift
adulate
adulation
adult
adulterer
adulterous
adultery
advance
advantage or
advantageous or
advantages or
advent
adventure/s /
adventurism
adventurous
adversary
adverse
adversity

advert
advertise/r /
advertisement or
advertising or
advice
advisable
advise
adviser/or
advisory
advocacy
advocate
aerate
aerator
aerial
aerobatics
aerobics
aerodrome
aerodynamics
aeroplane
aerosol
aerospace

aesthete
aesthetic
aesthetically or
affable
affair
affect
affectation
affection
affectionately
affective
affidavit
affiliate
affinity
affirm/ation /
affirmative
affix
afflict/ion / or
affluence or
affluent
afford
affray

affront ....

afield ....

afire ....

aflame ....

afloat ....

afoot ....

afore ....

aforementioned ....

aforesaid ....

afraid ....

after ....(b)(e)

after-dinner ....

after-effects ....

aftermath ....

afternoon ....

afterthought ....

afterwards ....

again ....

against ....

age ....

ageless ....

agency ....

agenda ....

agent ....

aggravate .... or ....

aggravation .... or ....

aggregate .... or ....

aggression .... or ....

aggressive .... or ....

aggrieve/d .... or .... / .... or ....

aghast ....

agile ....

agility .... or ....

ago ....

agony/ies .... / ....

agoraphobia ....

agree/d .... / ....

agreeable ....

agreement ....

agricultural ....

agriculture ....

aid ....

ail/ment .... / ....

aim ....

aimless ....

air ....(b)

airborne ....

air-condition/ing .... / ....

aircraft ....

airily .... or ....

airiness ....

airless ....

airline ....

airliner ....

airmail ....

airman ....

airmen ....

airport ....

air-stream ....

airy ....

aisle .... or ....

ajar ....

akin ....

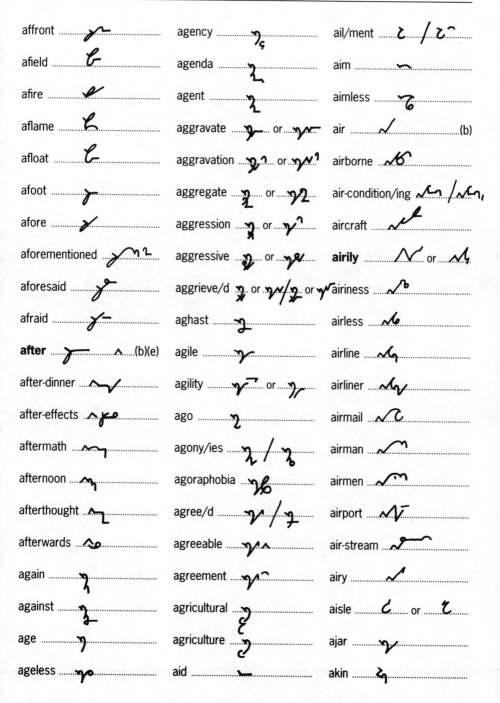

à la carte

alarm/ist

albeit

album

alcohol/ic

alcoholism

alcove

alderman

aldermen

ale

alert

algorithm

alias

alien/ate

alienation

alight

align/ment

alike

alimony

alive

alkaline

all

allay

allegation

allege

allegiance

allergic

allergy

alleviate

alley

alliance

allied

allocate

allocation

allot

allotment

allow/able

allowance

alloy

all-purpose

all-round/er

all-time

allude

allure

alluring

allusion

allusive

all-weather

ally

almanac

almond

almoner

almost

alms ... or ...

aloft

alone

along

alongside

aloof

aloud

alp

alphabet

alphabetical

alpha-numerical ....

alpine ....

already .... or ....

also ....

altar ....

alter ....

alteration ....

altercate ....

altercation ....

alternate ....

alternately ....

alternative/ly

alternator ....

although ....

altitude ....

altogether ....

aluminium ....

always ....

am ....

amalgamate ....

amalgamation ....

amass ....

amateur ....

amateurish ....

amateurism ....

amaze/d ....

amazement ....

ambassador ....

amber ....

ambidextrous ....

ambiguity ....

ambiguous ....

ambition ....

ambitious ....

ambivalent .... or ....

amble ....

ambulance ....

ambush ....

amenable ....

amend/ment ....

amenity ....

American ....

amethyst ....

amiable ....

amicable ....

amid ....

amiss ....

ammonia ....

amnesia ....

amnesty ....

amok ....

among ....

amongst ....

amount ....

amphetamine .... or ....

amphibian .... or ....

ample ....

amplification .... or ....

amplified ....

amplifier ....

amplify ....

amply ....

amputate ....

amuse/ment .... / ....
an ....
anagram ....
analog ....
analogical .... or ....
analogous ....
analogue ....
analogy .... or ....
analyse ....
analysis ....
analyst ....
analytic ....
analytical ....
anarchy ....
anatomy ....
ancestor ....
ancestral ....
ancestry ....
anchor ....
anchorage ....
anchorman ....

anchovy ....
ancient ....
ancillary .... or ....
and ....
anecdote ....
angel ....
anger ....
angle ....
anglican ....
angora ....
angrily ....
angry ....
anguish .... or ....
angular ....
animal ....
animate ....
animation ....
animator ....
animosity ....
ankle ....
anklebone .... or ....

anneal ....
annex ....
annihilate ....
annihilation ....
anniversary ....
annotate ....
annotation ....
announce/d .... / ....
announcement ....
announcer ....
annoy/ance .... / ....
annual ....
annuity ....
annul/ment ....
annunciate ....
annunciation ....
anomaly .... or ....
anonymity .... or ....
anonymous .... or .... or
anorak ....
another ....

answer/ed ....

answerable ....

antagonism ....

antagonist/ic ....

antagonize ....

antecede/nce ....

antecedent ....

antedate ....

antelope ....

antenna ....

anterior ....

ante-room ....

anthem .... or ....

anthology .... or ....

anthropologist ....

anthropology ....

anti-aircraft ....

antic ....

anticipate ....

anticipation ....

anticlimax ....

anti-clockwise ....

anticyclone ....

antidote ....

antifreeze ....

antiglare ....

antimissile ....

antipathetic ....

antipathy ....

Antipodes ....

antiquated ....

antique ....

antiquity ....

anti-social .... or ....

anti static ....

antonym .... or ....

anxiety ....

anxious/ly ....

any ....

anybody ....

anyhow ...., ... or ....

anyone ....

anything ....

anytime .... or ....

anyway ....

anywhere .... or ....

apart ....

apartheid ....

apartment ....

apathetic ....

apathy ....

ape ....

aperture ....

apex ....

apologetic ....

apologise ....

apology .... or ....

apostrophe ....

appalling ....

apparatus ....

apparel ....

apparent/ly ....

apparition ....

appeal
appear/ance
appease/ment
append/age
appendant
appendicular
appendix
appetiser
appetite
applaud
applause
apple
appliance
applicable
applicant
application
applicator
applied
apply
appoint/ment
apportion/ment

appraisal
appraise
appreciable
appreciate
appreciation
apprehend
apprehensible
apprehensive
apprentice ... or ...
apprenticeship ... or ...
approach/able
appropriate
appropriation
approval ... or ...
approve
approximate/ly
approximation
apricot
April ... , ... or ...
apron ... or ...
apropos

apt
aptitude
aqua
aquamarine
aquanaut
aquaplane
aquarium
aquarius
aquatic
aqueduct
arabic
arable
arbitrary
arbitrate
arbitration
arbitrator
arc
arcade
arch ... or ... (b)
archaeologist
archaeology

archaic
archangel
archbishop
archduke
archery
architect
architectural
architecture
architrave
archives ... or
arduous
are
area/s
arena
arguable
argue
argument
argumentative
arid
arise/n ... /
aristocracy ... or
aristocrat ... or
arithmetic
arm
armband ... or
armchair
armful
armistice
armour
army
aroma
aromatic
around ... or
arousal
arouse
arrange/ment ... /
array
arrear
arrest
arrival
arrive
arrogant
arrow ... or
arrowhead ... or
arsenic
arson
art
artefact
artichoke
article
articular
articulate
artifice
artificial
artificiality
artisan
artist
artistic/ally ... /
artistry
as
asbestos
ascend
ascendant/ent

ascender
ascension
ascent
ascertain
ascribe
ashamed
ashen
ashore
aside
ask
asked
askew
asleep
asparagus
aspect/s
asperity ... or ...
asphalt ... or ...
asphyxia
asphyxiate
aspirant
aspirate

aspiration
aspirator
aspire
aspirin
aspiring
assassin
assassinate
assassination
assault/ed
assay
assemble
assembly
assent
assert/ion
assertive
assess/ment
assessor
assets
assiduous
assign
assignee

assignment
assignor
assimilate
assimilation
assist
assistance
assistant ... or ...
assize
associate
association ... or ... (g)
associative
assort/ment
assuasive ... or ...
assume
assumption ... or ...
assumptive ... or ...
assurance
assure/d
astern
astonish/ed
astonishment

astound
astray
astride
astringent
astrologer
astrology
astronaut
astronomer
astronomy
astute
asunder
asylum
at
ate
athlete
athletics
atlas
atmosphere
atmospherics
atom
atomic or (g)

atomizer
atone/ment
attach
attaché
attachment
attack/er
attain/able
attainment
attempt
attend
attendance
attendant
attention or
attentive
attest
attestant
attestation
attic
attire
attitude
attorney

attract/ion
attractive
attribute
attribution
aubergine
auction
auctioneer
audacity
audible
audience
audio
audition
auditor
auditorium
augment/ation
August
aunt or
auspice
auspicious
austere
austerity or

authentic
authenticate
authenticity
author
authoritarian
authoritative
authority (g)
authorize
authorship
auto or (b)
autobahn
autobiography
autoclave
autocrat
autograph
automated
automatic/ally
automation
automobile
autonomous
autonomy

autumn
auxiliary
avail/able
avalanche
avenge
avenue or
average
averse
aversion
avert
aviary
aviation
aviator
avid
avocado
avoid/ance
avow/ed
await
awake/n or
award
aware/ness

awash
away
awe
awesome
awful
awhile
awkward or
awning
awoke
awry or
axe
axis
axle
Axminster
ayatollah
azalea or
azure or

baby

babysitter

bachelor

back

back-dated

background ... or ...

back-lash

back-log

back-rest

backwards

bacon

bacteria

bad/ly ... or ...

badge

badminton

baffle

bag

baggage

baguette

bail

bailiff

baize ... or ...

bake

baker

bakery

balance

balcony

ball

ballad

ballerina ... or ...

ballet

ballistic

balloon

ballpoint

balustrade

ban

banana

band

bandit

bang

bangle

banister

bank

banker

banking

bankrupt

bankruptcy

banned

banns

banquet

bar/bare

barbecue ... or ...

barely

bargain

baritone

bark
barometer
barracks
barred
barrel
barren
barricade
barrier … or …
barrister
base/ment
bash/ful
basic/ally … or …
basis … or …
bask
basket
basketball
bat
batch
bath/bathe
bathroom
batter

battle
battleship
bay
bazaar
be
beach
beam
bean
bear/er
beard
beast/ly … or …
beat
Beaufort scale
beautician
beautiful/ly
beauty
became
because … or …
become
bed
bedazzle

bedlam
bedroom
bedside
bedsitter
bedspread
bee/s
beef
beefburger … or …
been … or … (g)
beetroot
before
beforehand
began
beggar
begin
beginner
beginning
begrudge
behalf
behave
behaviour

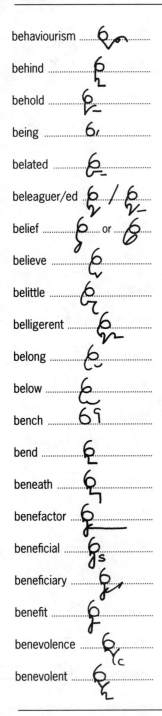

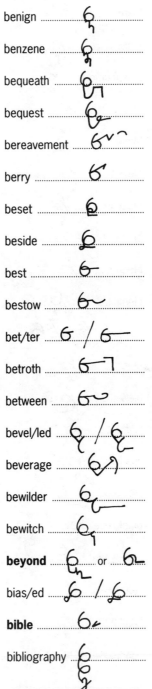

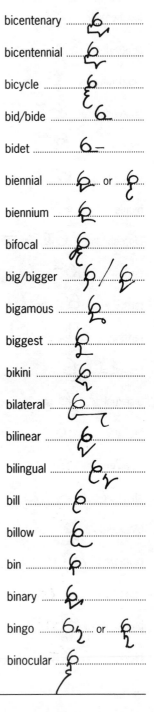

behaviourism
behind
behold
being
belated
beleaguer/ed ... /
belief ... or
believe
belittle
belligerent
belong
below
bench
bend
beneath
benefactor
beneficial
beneficiary
benefit
benevolence
benevolent

benign
benzene
bequeath
bequest
bereavement
berry
beset
beside
best
bestow
bet/ter ... /
betroth
between
bevel/led ... /
beverage
bewilder
bewitch
beyond ... or
bias/ed ... /
bible
bibliography

bicentenary
bicentennial
bicycle
bid/bide
bidet
biennial ... or
biennium
bifocal
big/bigger ... /
bigamous
biggest
bikini
bilateral
bilinear
bilingual
bill
billow
bin
binary
bingo ... or
binocular

biochemistry
biographer
biography
biological
biologist
biology
bionic
biotechnology or
bird
birth or
birthday or
biscuit
bisexual
bit/bite
bizarre
black/er /
blackest
blame/ful /
blanch
blank
blanket

blare
blasé
blasphemous
blast
blatant
blaze
bleach
bleed
bleep
blemish
blend/er /
bless
blew
blight
blind
blitz
block/age /
bloodshed
bloom
blossom
blouse or

blouson
bludgeoned
blue
bluebell or
blueprint
bluff
blunder
blunt
blush
blusher
bluster/y /
board
boardroom
boast/ful /
boat
bodily
body
bodywork
bogus
boil
boisterous/ness /

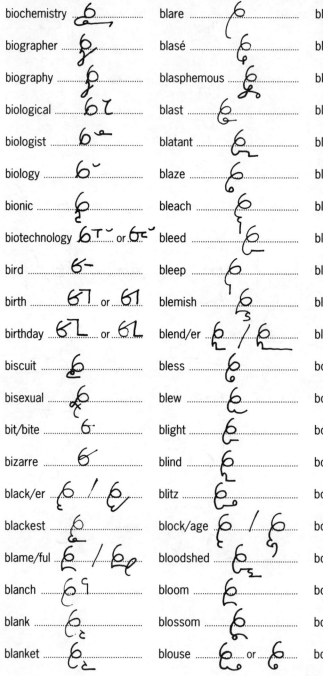

- bold
- boldface ... or ...
- bollard ... or ...
- bolt
- bomb
- bombard
- bombastic
- bombshell
- bona fide
- bon appetit
- bond
- bondage
- bone
- bonfire
- bonus/es
- bon voyage
- boo
- book
- book-keeper ... or ...
- boon
- boost
- boot/s ... or ...
- border
- borderline
- bored
- boredom
- born
- borough
- borrow/er
- bosom
- boss/y
- botanical
- botanist
- botany
- both
- bother
- bothersome
- bottle
- bottom
- bough
- bought
- boulevard
- bounce/d
- bound/ary
- boutique
- bowl/er
- box/er
- boy/buoy
- boycott
- boyfriend ... or ...
- boyhood
- boyish
- bra
- bracelet
- bracket
- brag
- braid
- Braille
- brain
- brainwashed
- braise
- bramble
- branch

brand
brandish
brand-new
brandy
brass
brave/ly
bravery
breach
bread
breadcrumbs
break/able
breakdown
breakfast
breath/breathe
breathalyse/r
breathtaking
breeze
brevity ... or ...
brewer/y
bribe/ry
brick

bricklayer
bride
bridegroom
bridesmaid
bridge
brief ... or ...
brief-case
brigade
bright/en
brightness
brilliance
brilliant
bring
brisk
Britain
Britannia
British
Briton
brittle
broad
broadcast

broccoli
brochure
broke/n
broker
bronze ... or ...
bros.
broth
brother
brought
brown
browse
brunette
brush ... or ...
brushes ... or ...
brusque
brutal/ly
brutality ... or ...
brute
bubble
bubbly
bucket

budget ....

buff ....

buffet .... or ....

buggy ....

build/er ..... / .....

bulk ....

bull ....

bulldozer ....

bulletin ....

bullion ....

bump/er ..... / .....

bunch ....

bundle ....

bungalow ....

bunk/er ..... / .....

buoyancy ....

buoyant ....

burdensome ....

bureau ....

bureaucracy .... or ....

bureaucrat .... or ....

bureaucratic .... or ....

burglar ....

burgle ....

buried ....

burly ....

burn ....

burst ....

bury ....

bus/es ..... / .....

bush/es ..... / .....

bushy ....

business .... or ....

businessman .... or ....

busy ....

but ....

butcher ....

butter ....

butterfly ....

button ....

buttonhole .... or ....

buyer ....

buzzer ....

by/buy ....

by-election ....

bygone ....

by-law ....

bypass ....

byte ....

cab ... or ...

cabaret

cabbage

cabinet ... or ...

cable

cache

cactus

cadence

cadet

café

cafeteria

caffeine

caftan

cage

cajole

cake

calcium ... or ...

calculable

calculate

calculation

calculator ... or ...

calendar

calibrate

call

caller

calligraphy

calm

calmness

calorie ... or ...

camber

came

camel

cameo

camera

camouflage

camp/er

campaign

campus

can

canal

cancel ... or ...

cancellation ... or ...

cancer

candidate

candidature

candelabra

candy

canine

cannot

canopy

can't

cantankerous ... or ...

canteen

cantilever

canvas

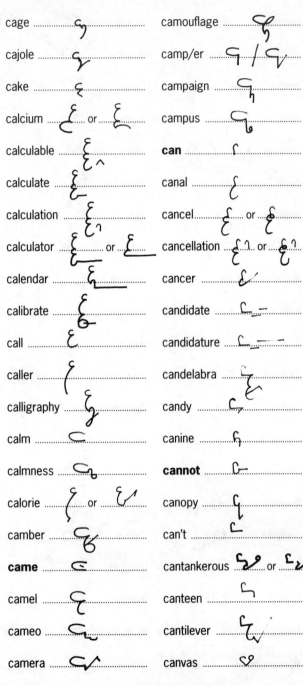

capability
capable
capably
capacious
capacity
capital
capitalize
capitation
capitulate
capsule
captain
caption
captive
car
carafe
caravan
carbohydrate
carbon
carbonate
carburettor
card

cardboard
cardigan
cardinal
care
carefree
career
careful/ly
careless/ly
carelessness
caretaker
cargo
carnage
carnival
carnivorous
car park
carpenter
carpet
carriage
carriageway
carry
carton

cartoon
cartridge
carve
case
cash
cashier
casino
casserole
cassette
casualty
catalogue
catastrophe
catastrophic
catch
category or
categorical
caterer
catering
cathedral
catholic
cattle

caught

cauliflower

cause

caution/ary /

cave

cavity

cayenne

cease/less /

Ceefax

celebrate

celebration

celebrity

cellophane

cellulite

celluloid

cellulose

Celsius

cement

cemetery

censor or

censorship or

census

cent

centenarian

centenary

centigrade

centimetre

central

centre

century or

cereal

ceremony

certain

certainly

certainty

certificate

certified

certify

cessation

chain

chair

chairman

chairmanship

chalet

chalk

chalkboard

challenge

challenger

chamber

Chamber of Commerce

champagne

champion/ship /

chance/d /

Chancellor

Chancellor of the Exchequer

change or

changeable

changeless

changeover

channel

chap

chapel

chapter

character

characteristic

charge

chargeable

charisma

charity ... or ...

charitable

charm

chart

charter

chase

chassis

chastise

château

chatter

chauffeur

cheap

check

checklist

checkmate

check-out ... or ...

cheek/y ... or ...

cheer

cheerful/ly

cheerfulness

cheerless

cheerlessness

cheese

cheesecake

chef

chemical

chemist

chemistry

cheque

cheque book ... or ...

cherry

chest

chew

chicken

chief/ly ... or ...

child

childbirth

childhood ... or ...

children

chill/y

chimes

chimney

china

Chinese

chipolata

chisel ... or ...

chloride ... or ...

chlorinate ... or ...

chlorine ... or ...

chlorophyll ... or ...

chocolate

choice ... or ...

choke/d

chop

chopsticks

choral ... or ...

chore

choreographer
chorus
chosen
Christian
Christmas
chrome ... or ...
chromium ... or ...
chromosome ... or ...
chronic ... or ...
chronicle ... or ...
chronological ... or ...
chubby
chuck
chug
chum
church
churlish/ly
chutney
cider
cigar
cigarette

cinder
cinema
circa
circle
circuit
circular
circulate
circulation
circumference
circumscribe
circumspect
circumstance
circumstantial
circumvent
circus
cistern
citizens
citizenship
citric
city (g)
civic

civil
civilization
civilized
clad/ding
claim
clairvoyance ... or ...
clairvoyant ... or ...
clap
clarification ... or ...
clarify ... or ...
class
classic/al
classified ... or ...
classify ... or ...
classroom
clause
claustrophobia
clay
clean/er
cleanse
clear

clearance
clearer
clearing
clearly
clement
clergy
clergyman
clerical
clerk ... or ...
clever/ly
cliché
client/èle
climate
climax
climb
clinch
cling
clinic
clinical
clinician
clock

clockwise
cloister
close
closure
cloth/clothe
cloud
clown
club
clue/less
clumsily
clumsiness
clumsy
cluster/ed
clutter
coagulate
coal
coalition
coarse
coast
coastguard
coat

cobble
cobweb
cocktail
cocoa
codicil
co-educational
co-exist
coexistence
coffee
cognizance
coherence
coherent
coiffure
coincide ... or ...
coincidence ... or ...
colander
cold/er
coleslaw
collaborate
collaboration
collapse

collapsible/able

collar

collate

collator

collateral

colleague

collect/or

collection

college

collide

collision

collusion

colony

colour/ful

column

columnist

comb

combat

combination ... or ...

combine/d

combustible

combustion ... or ...

come

comeback

comedy

comfort

comfortable

comic/al

comma

command/er

commandment

commemorate

commemoration

commence/ment

commend/able

commensurate

comment

commentate

commerce

commercial/ly

commiserate

commission/er

commit/ment

committee ... or ... (g)

commodity

common

commonplace

commonsense

commonwealth

communal

commune

communicate

communication

communiqué

community

commuter

compact

companion

company ... or ... (g)

comparable

comparability

comparative/ly

compare

comparison

compass

compassion/ate

compatible

compel

compensate

compensation

competent

competition

competitive

competitors

compile

complacence

complacency

complacent

complain

complainant

complained

complaint

complement

complementary

complete

complex

complexity ... or ...

complication

compliment/ary

comply

component

compose

compost

comprehend

comprehension

comprehensive

compress

compression

compressor

compromise

compulsory

computation

compute

computer

computerized

comrade/ship

conceal ... or ...

conceit ... or ...

conceivable

conceive

concentrate

concentration

concept/ion

concern

concert

concession

concessionary

conciliation

conciliatory

concise

conclude

conclusion

conclusive

concoct

concord

concourse

concrete
concur
concurrence
concurrent
concussion
condemn
condemnation
condensation
condense
condescend
condition/al
condolence
condominium
condone
conducive
conduct/or
confectioner/y
confederation
confer
conference
confess/ion

confessional
confidence
confident
confidential
configuration
confine/ment
confirm ... or
confirmation ... or
confiscate
conflict
conform ... or
confront
confrontation
confuse
confusion
congenial
congest/ion
conglomerate
conglomeration
congratulate ... or
congratulations

congregate ... or
congress
congressman
conjure/r
connect/ion
connivance
connive
connoisseur
connote
connotation
conquer
conscience ... or
conscientious ... or
conscious/ly ... or
consecrate
consecutive
consensus
consequence ... or
consequent/ly
consequential
conservation

conservative
conservatory
conserve
consider
considerable
considerably
consideration
consign/ment
consist
consistency
consistent/ly
consolation
console
consolidate
consolidation
consortium ... or ...
conspicuous
conspicuously
conspiracy
constant/ly
constellation

consternation
constituency
constituent
constitute
constitution
constraint
construct/ion
constructive
construe
consult/ancy
consultant ... or ...
consume/r
consumption ... or ...
contact
contagious
contain/er
contaminate
contamination
contemporary
contempt ... or ...
contend

contentious
content
contention
contentment
contest
continent/al
contingency
contingent
continual/ly
continuance
continue
continuity
continuous
continuously
contortion
contraception
contraceptive
contract
contraction
contractual
contradict/ion

contralto
contrary
contrast
contravene
contravention
contribute
contribution
contributor
contributory
contrition
contrivance
contrive
control
controversial
controversy
convalesce/nt
convene/r
convenience
convenient
conveniently ... or ...
convent

convention
converge
conversant
conversation
converse
conversion
convert
convey
conveyance
convict/ion
convince
convivial
cook/ed
cooker/y
cool/er
co-operate
co-operation
co-operative
co-ordinate
co-ordination
copper

copy
copyright
cord
cordial/ly
cordiality ... or ...
cork
corn
corner
cornice ... or ...
coroner
corporation
correct/ly
correction
correspond/ence
correspondent ... or ...
correspondingly
corridor
corroboration
corroborative
corrode
corrupt/ion

cosmetics

cosmonaut

cosmopolitan

cost/ly /

costume

cottage

cotton

cough

could

council or

councillor

counsel

counsellor

count

countenance c

counter (b)

counterfeit

counterfoil

counterpart

countersign

countries

country

countryside

county

couple

coupon

courage

courageous

courgette

courier

course

court

courteous

courtesy

cousin

covenant

cover

cow

coward/ly /

cox

coy

crab

crack or

cracker or

cradle

craft/y /

craftsman

craftsmanship

crag

cramp

crane

crank

crash

crater

crave or

craze

cream

create

creation

creative

creature

crèche

credentials

credibility

credit

credit card ... or ...

creditor

creditworthy

credulous

cremation

crescent

crevice

crew

cricket

crime

criminal/s

cringe ... or ...

crinkle ... or ...

cripple

crisis ... or ...

criteria

criterion

critic

critical/ly

criticism

criticize ... or ...

croissant

crop

croquette

cross ... or ...

crossed ... or ...

cross-examination ... or ...

cross-examine ... or ...

cross-over ..., ... or ...

crossroads

crossword

crowd

crown

crucial/ly

crude

cruel

cruelty

cruise

crumb

crumble

crumple

crush

crutch ... or ...

cry

crypt

cucumber

cuisine

culinary

culottes

culprit

cultivate

cultivation

cultural

culture

cumbersome

cumulative

cup

cupboard

curator

curb

curd

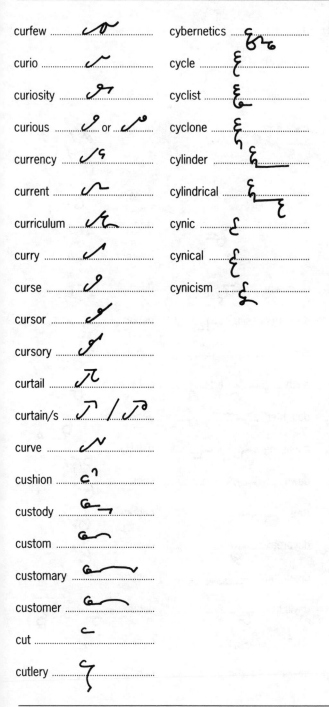

curfew ....

curio ....

curiosity ....

curious .... or ....

currency ....

current ....

curriculum ....

curry ....

curse ....

cursor ....

cursory ....

curtail ....

curtain/s .... / ....

curve ....

cushion ....

custody ....

custom ....

customary ....

customer ....

cut ....

cutlery ....

cybernetics ....

cycle ....

cyclist ....

cyclone ....

cylinder ....

cylindrical ....

cynic ....

cynical ....

cynicism ....

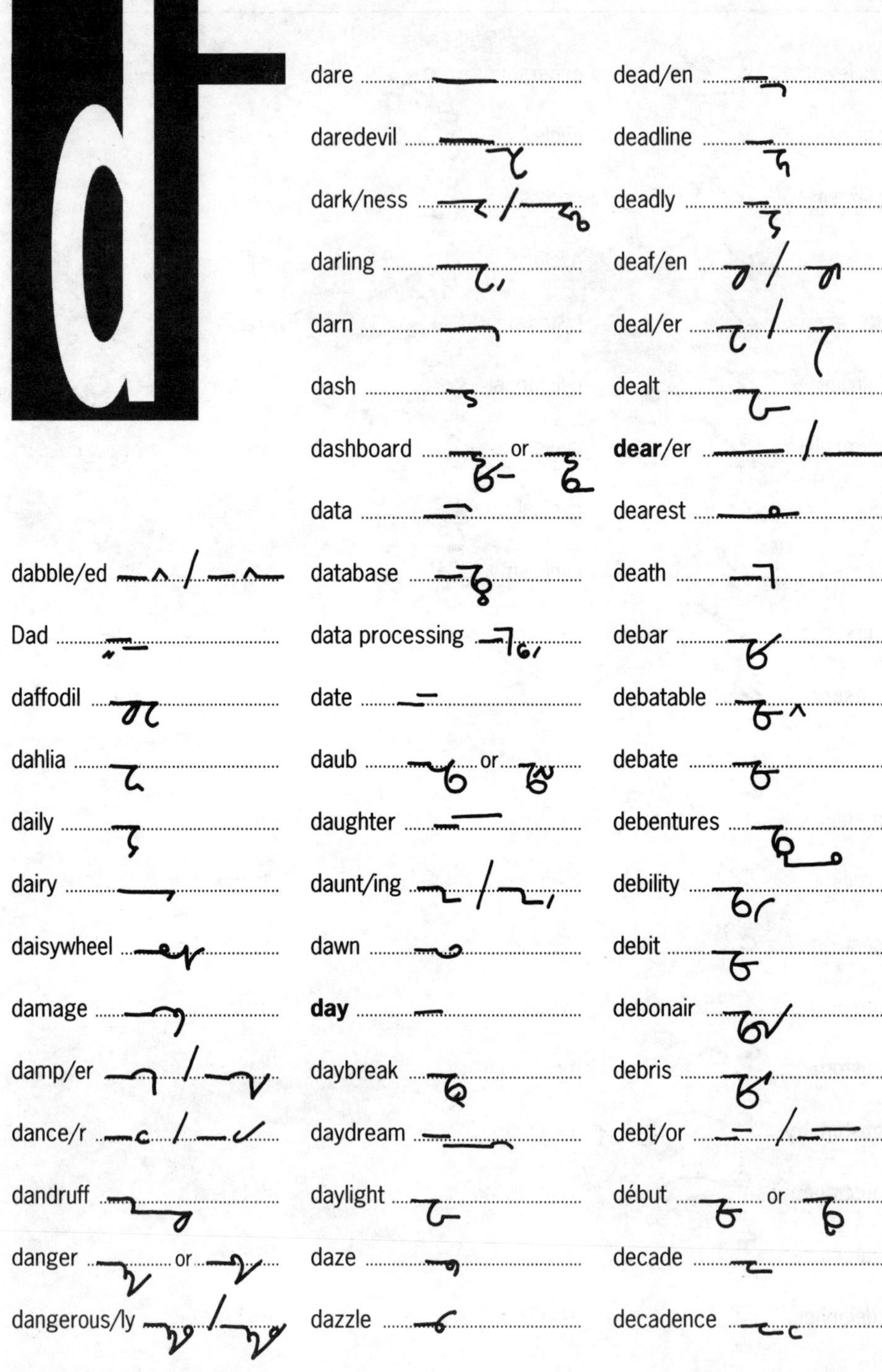

d

dabble/ed
Dad
daffodil
dahlia
daily
dairy
daisywheel
damage
damp/er
dance/r
dandruff
danger ... or ...
dangerous/ly

dare
daredevil
dark/ness
darling
darn
dash
dashboard ... or ...
data
database
data processing
date
daub ... or ...
daughter
daunt/ing
dawn
day
daybreak
daydream
daylight
daze
dazzle

dead/en
deadline
deadly
deaf/en
deal/er
dealt
dear/er
dearest
death
debar
debatable
debate
debentures
debility
debit
debonair
debris
debt/or
début ... or ...
decade
decadence

decanter ....
decay ....
deceased .... or ....
deceit .... or ....
deceitful .... or ....
deceive ....
decelerate ....
December ....
decency ....
decent .... or ....
deception ....
deceptive ....
decibels ....
decide ....
decidedly .... or ....
decision ....
decisive ....
decimal .... or ....
decimalization .... or ....
decimate .... or ....
decipher ....

deck ....
declaration ....
declare ....
decline ....
decompose ....
decompress ....
decompression ....
decongestant ....
decorate ....
decorations ....
decorum ....
decoy ....
decrease ....
decree ....
decrepit ....
dedicate ....
dedication ....
deduce .... or ....
deduct/ion ....
deed ....
deep/en ....

deface ....
defamation ....
defamatory ....
defame ....
default ....
defeat ....
defect/ion ....
defective ....
defence/less ....
defend/ant ....
defensible ....
defensive ....
defer ....
deference ....
deferential ....
defiance ....
defiant ....
deficiency ....
deficient ....
deficit ....
define/d ....

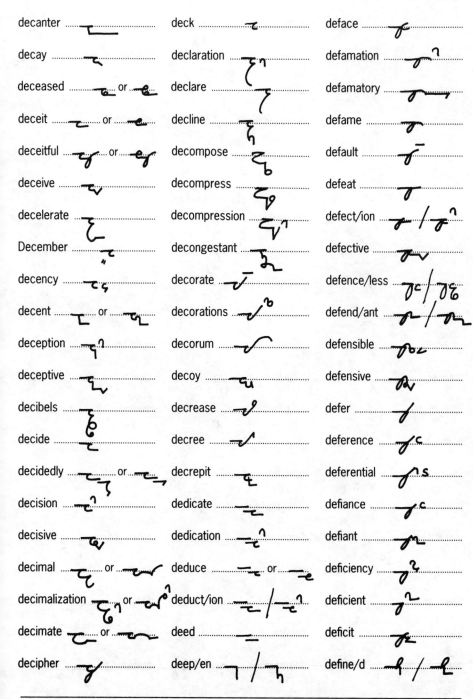

definite
definitely ... or ...
definition
deflate
deformity
defrost
defunct ... or ...
defy ... or ...
degenerate
degradation
degrade
degree
dehydrate
deity
dejected
delay
delectable
delegate
delegation
delete
deletion

deliberate/ly
delicacy
delicate
delicatessen
delicious ... or ...
delight/ful
delineate
delinquency
delinquent
deliver/y ... or ...
deluge
delusion
de luxe
delve
demand
demarcate
demarcation
demeanour
demented
demise
democracy ... or ...

democrat
democratic/ally
demolish
demolition
demonstrate
demonstration
demonstrative
demoralize
demote
demure
denial
denied
denims
denomination
denominator
denote
denounce
dense
density
dent
dentist

denture
denunciation
deny
deodorant
depart
department or
departmental or
departure
depend
dependant/ent
deplete
deplorable
deplore
deploy/ment /
deport/ation /
deportment
deposit
deposition
depot
deprave
depravity

deprecate
depreciate
depreciation
depress
deprivation
deprive
depth
deputy
derelict
derisory
derive
derivative
derogatory
DERV
descend
descendant
descent
describe
description
descriptive
desert

deserve
design
designation
desirable/ability
desire
desk
desolate
despair
despatched
desperation
despicable
despise
despite
dessert
destination
destined
destiny
destitute
destitution
destroy
destruct/ion /

destructive
detach/ment
detail
detain
detect
detective
detector
detention
deter
detergent
deteriorate ... or ...
deterioration
determination
determine
deterrent
detest/able
detour
detract/ion
detriment/al
devaluate
devalue

devastate
develop/ed ... or ...
development
deviation
device
devil
devise
devious
devoid
devote
devotion
devour
dexterity
dexterous
diabolical
diagnose
diagnosis ... or ...
diagonal
diagram
dial
dialogue

diameter
diamonds
diary
dice ... or ...
Dictaphone
dictate
dictator
dictatorial
dictatorship
dictionary
did
die
diet
differ
difference
different/ly
differential
differentiate
differentiation
difficult/y
diffidence

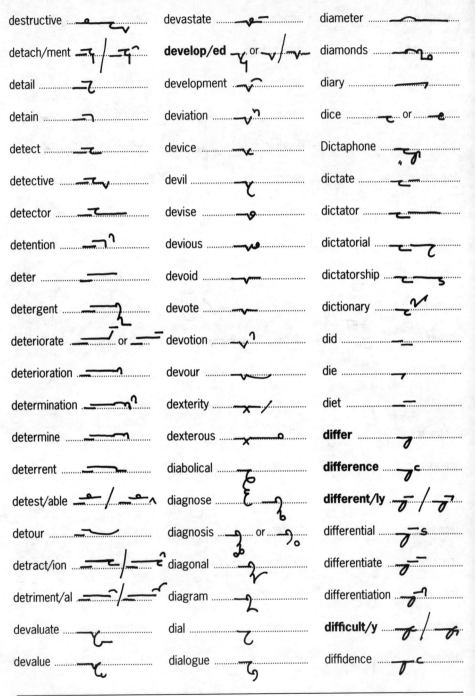

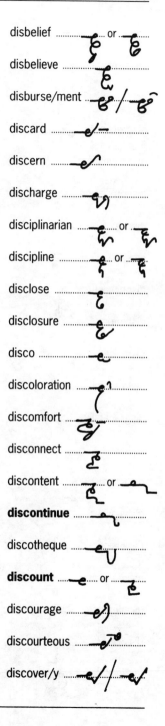

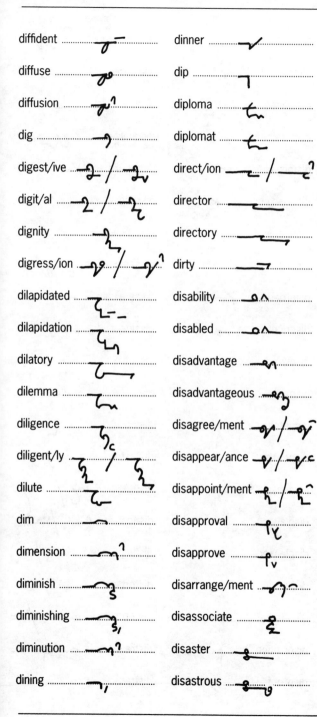

diffident
diffuse
diffusion
dig
digest/ive
digit/al
dignity
digress/ion
dilapidated
dilapidation
dilatory
dilemma
diligence
diligent/ly
dilute
dim
dimension
diminish
diminishing
diminution
dining

dinner
dip
diploma
diplomat
direct/ion
director
directory
dirty
disability
disabled
disadvantage
disadvantageous
disagree/ment
disappear/ance
disappoint/ment
disapproval
disapprove
disarrange/ment
disassociate
disaster
disastrous

disbelief ... or
disbelieve
disburse/ment
discard
discern
discharge
disciplinarian ... or
discipline ... or
disclose
disclosure
disco
discoloration
discomfort
disconnect
discontent ... or
discontinue
discotheque
discount ... or
discourage
discourteous
discover/y

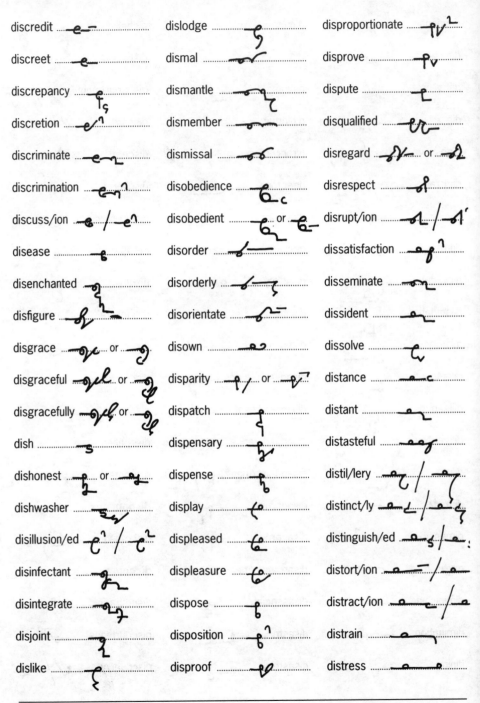

discredit
discreet
discrepancy
discretion
discriminate
discrimination
discuss/ion
disease
disenchanted
disfigure
disgrace
disgraceful
disgracefully
dish
dishonest
dishwasher
disillusion/ed
disinfectant
disintegrate
disjoint
dislike
dislodge
dismal
dismantle
dismember
dismissal
disobedience
disobedient
disorder
disorderly
disorientate
disown
disparity
dispatch
dispensary
dispense
display
displeased
displeasure
dispose
disposition
disproof
disproportionate
disprove
dispute
disqualified
disregard
disrespect
disrupt/ion
dissatisfaction
disseminate
dissident
dissolve
distance
distant
distasteful
distil/lery
distinct/ly
distinguish/ed
distort/ion
distract/ion
distrain
distress

distribute

distribution

distributor

district

disturb

disturbance

disused

ditch

dive

diverse

diversion

divert

divide

dividend or (g)

divine

division

divorce

divorcee

do

dock

doctor

doctrinaire

doctrine

document

documentary

documentation

does

dog

dogmatic

dogmatism

doing

dollar

domain

domestic

domesticity

domicile

domiciliary

dominate

dominion

domino

donation

done

donkey

door

doorway

dormant

dormitory

dossier

dot

double

double-glazing

doubt

doubtful

doubtless

dough

doughnut

dove

dovetail

down

downcast or

downpour

downstairs

downstream

downward
dozen
draft
drag
drain
drama
dramatic
drank
drastic
draughty
draughtsman
draw
drawback ... or
drawer
drawn
dread
dreadful/ly
dream
dreamer
dreamily
dreamy

dress/es
dresser
dried
drift
driftwood
drill
drink/er
drive/r
dromedary
drop
drought
drown
drudgery
drug
drum
drummer
drumsticks
drunk
drunkard
drunken
dry

dubious ... or
duck
due
duet
dumb
dumbfound
dungaree
duplex
duplicate
duplicator
durable
duration
during
dusk
dust
dustbin ... or
dutiful
duty
duty-free
duvet
dwarf

dwindle ....

dye ....

dyed ....

dynamics ....

dynamite ....

dynamo ....

dyslexia ....

dyslexic ....

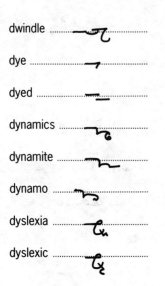

e

each .... or ....

eager/ly........ / ....

ear ....

earmark ....

earlier ....

earliest ....

early ....

earn ....

earnings ....

ear-ring ....

earth ....

earthenware .... or ....

earthly .... or ....

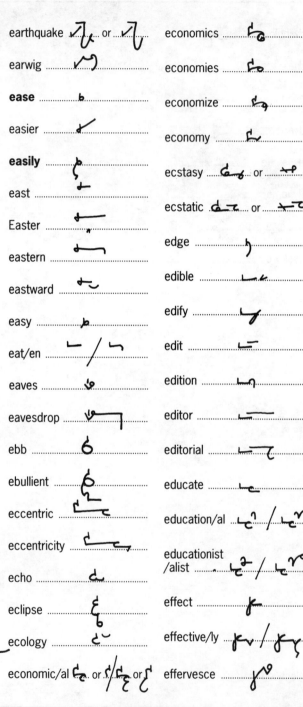

earthquake .... or ....

earwig ....

ease ....

easier ....

easily ....

east ....

Easter ....

eastern ....

eastward ....

easy ....

eat/en .... / ....

eaves ....

eavesdrop ....

ebb ....

ebullient ....

eccentric ....

eccentricity ....

echo ....

eclipse ....

ecology ....

economic/al .... or .... / .... or ....

economics ....

economies ....

economize ....

economy ....

ecstasy .... or ....

ecstatic .... or ....

edge ....

edible ....

edify ....

edit ....

edition ....

editor ....

editorial ....

educate ....

education/al .... / ....

educationist /alist .... / ....

effect ....

effective/ly .... / ....

effervesce ....

effervescent

efficiency

efficient/ly

effluent

effort

effortless

egg/s

ego

eight ... or ...

either

elaborate

elaboration

elapse

elastic

elasticity

elated

elation

elbow

elder/ly

eldest

elect/ion

elective

electoral

electorate

electric ... (b)

electrical

electrician

electricity ... or ...

electrification

electrocute

electrode

electrolysis

electron ... or ...

electronic

electroplate

elegance

elegant

element

elemental

elementary

elephant

elevate

elevation

elevator

elicit

eligible

eliminate

elimination

élite

ellipsis

elm

elocution

elongate

elope

eloquence

else

elsewhere

elucidate

elude

elusive

emaciate

emancipate

embalm

embargo
embark/ation
embarrass
embarrassment
embassy
embezzle
emblem
embodied
embolden
emboss
embrace or
embrocation
embroidery
embryonic or
emerald
emerge
emergency
emigrant
emigrate
eminence
eminent/ly

emission
emotion
emotionally
empathy
emphasize
emphatic/ally
empirical
employ
employee
employer
employment
empower
emptiness
empty
emulate
emulation
enable
enact or
enamour
enchant or
encircle or

enclose/d
enclosure or
encompass
encore or
encounter
encourage/ment
encroach
encumbrance
encyclopaedia
end
ended
endearment
endeavour
endless/ly
endocrine
endorse/ment
endow/ment
endurance
endure
enemy
energetic

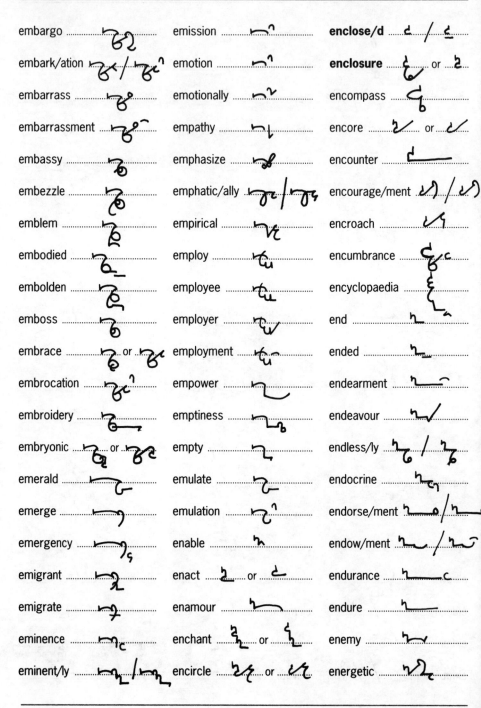

energy
enforce/ment
engage/ment
engine
engineer
English or
engraving
engross
enigma
enigmatic
enjoy
enjoyment
enlarge
enlargement
enlighten/ment
enlist or
enormous/ly
enough
enquire/s or
enquiries or
enquiry or

enrage
enrol/ment
en route
ensemble
ensue
en suite
ensure
entail
entangle
enter/s
enterprise
entertain/er
entertainment
enthral
enthuse or
enthusiasm or
enthusiastic or
enthusiastically or
entire/ly
entitled
entity

entrance
entrée
entrepreneur
entries
entry
enumerate
enumeration
enumerator
enunciate
envelope
environment
environmental
envisage
envoy
envy
epic
epidemic
epilogue
episode
epitaph
epitomize

epoch

equal

equality

equate

equation

equator

equestrian

equilateral

equilibrium or

equip

equipment

equitable

equities

equivalent

equivocal

eradicate

erase

eraser

erect/ion /

ergonomics

erode

erosion

errand

erratic

erroneous

error

erudite

erupt/ion /

escalate

escalation

escalator

escapade

escape

escort

especial/ly /

espionage

essay

essence or

essential/ly /

establish or

establishment or

estate

esteem

estimate

estrange or

etc.

etching

eternal

eternity

ethical

ethics

ethnic

ethos or

etiquette

etymology

euphoria

Europe

European

evacuate

evacuation

evade

evaluate

evaluation

evaporate
evaporation
evasive
eve
even
evening
event
eventual/ly / or
eventuality or
ever or (b)
evergreen or
ever-increasing
everlasting
ever-loving
evermore
every
everybody
everyone
everything
everywhere or
evict/ion /

evidence or
evident/ly /
evil
evoke
evolution
evolve
ewe
ewer
exacerbate
exact
exactly or
exam
examination
examine/r /
example or
exasperate
excavate
excavations
exceed
exceeding/ly /
excel or

excellence or
excellent or
except/ion /
exceptional/ly /
excerpt or
excess
excessive/ly /
exchange or
exchequer or
excise
excitable or
excite or
excitedly or
excitement or
exclaim
exclamation
exclude
exclusive/ly /
excommunicate or
excruciating
excursion

excuse ....

execrable ....

executive ....

executor ....

exemplary .... or ....

exempt .... or ....

exercise/s .... / ....

exert/ion .... / ....

exhaust/ion .... or .... / ....

exhaustive .... or ....

exhibit/ion .... / ....

exhibitionist ....

exhilarate .... or ....

exhort ....

exile ....

exist ....

existence ....

exonerate ....

exorbitant .... or ....

exorcise ....

exorcist ....

exotic .... or ....

expand ....

expanse ....

expansion ....

expect/ing .... or .... / ....

expectations ....

expedient ....

expedite ....

expedition ....

expeditionary ....

expel ....

expulsion ....

expend ....

expenditure ....

expense ....

expensive ....

experience ....

experiment ....

experimental/ly .... / ....

expert ....

expertise ....

expire ....

explain ....

explanation ....

explanatory ....

explicable ....

explicit ....

explode ....

explosion ....

exploit ....

exploration ....

explore ....

explosive ....

exponent ....

export/er .... / ....

expose ....

exposure ....

express ....

expression ....

expressive ....

expropriate ....

expulsion ....

exquisite

extempore

extend

extension

extensive/ly

extent

extenuate

exterior

exterminate

external/ly

extinct

extinguish

extinguisher

extortion

extortionate

extra

extract/ion

extradition

extramural

extraneous

extraordinary

extravagance

extravagant

extravaganza

extreme/ly

extricate

extrovert

exuberant

eye/s

eyebrow

eyeing

eyelash

eyesight

eyewitness

fable

fabric

fabricate

fabulous

façade

face

facet

facetious ... or ...

facial

facile

facility ... or ...

facsimile

fact

faction

factor

factory

factual

faculty

fade

Fahrenheit ... or ...

fail

failure

faint

fair

fairground

fairly

fairness

fait accompli

faith

faithful ... or ...

faithfully ... or ...

fake

fall/en

fallacy

fallible

false/ly

falsify

falter

familiar

familiarity

familiarization

family

famine

famous/ly

fan

fanatic/al

fanbelt

fancied

fancy

fanfare

fangs

fantastic

fantastically

fantasy

far

farce

fares

farewell

farm

farmer

farmhouse

far-off

farther

farthest

fascia

fascinate or

fascination or

fascism

fashion

fashionable

fashionably

fast/er /

fastened

fastest

fastidious

fat

fatal/ly /

fatality or

fate

fateful

father

fatherhood

fathom

fatigue

fatuous

fault/y /

faultless

favour/able /

favoured

favourite

fax

fear/ful /

fearless

fearsome

feasible

feasibility

feast

feather

feature/less /

February

feckless

fed

federal

federation

fee

feeble

feed

feel/ings /

feelingly

feet

feign

fell

fellow

fellowship

felon/y /

felt

female

feminine

femininity
fence
fend
ferment/ation /
ferocious
ferry
fertile
fertility or
fervent
festival
festive
festivity or
fetch
fête
feud
feudal
fever
feverish
few/er or /
fiancé
fiancée

fiasco
fibres
fibrous
fickle
fiction
fictional
fiddle
fidelity or
fidget
field
fiendish
fierce
fiery
fifth
fig
fight
figure
figurehead
figurine
file
filigree

fill
fillet
fillip
film
filter
filthy
final
finalist
finality or
finance
financial
financier
find
fine
finesse
finger
fingerprint or
fingertips
finish or
fir
fire

fire escape ....

fireplace .... or ....

fireside ....

firewood ....

firework ....

firm ....

firmly .... or ....

firmness ....

first ....

first aid ....

first-class ....

first-hand ....

first-rate ....

fiscal ....

fish ....

fisherman ....

fit/ter .... / ....

fitness ....

fitting/ly .... / ....

five ....

fix ....

fixative ....

fixture ....

flabbergast ....

flabby ....

flag ....

flagrant .... or ....

flagstone ....

flake ....

flamboyant ....

flame ....

flammable ....

flan ....

flank ....

flannel ....

flap ....

flare ....

flash ....

flashback ....

flat ....

flat-iron ....

flat rate ....

flavour ....

flaw ....

fleece ....

fleecy ....

fleet ....

flesh ....

flew ....

flex/ible .... / ....

flexibility ....

flicker ....

flight ....

flimsy ....

flinch ....

fling ....

flirt .... or ....

float ....

flock ....

flood ....

floodlight ....

floor ....

floppy ....

floppy disk ....

floral ....

florist ....

flotilla ....

flounce ....

flounder ....

flourish ....

flower ....

flowerbeds ....

flown ....

fluctuate ....

fluctuation ....

fluent ....

fluorescent ....

fluoride ....

flush ....

fluster ....

fly/er ....

flying squad ....

fly over ....

focus ....

focused ....

foe ....

fog/gy ....

foible ....

fold ....

foliage ....

folk ....

folklore ....

follow ....

fond ....

fondness ....

food ....

fool ....

foolish ....

foolproof ....

foot ....

football ....

footprint ....

footsteps ....

for ....

forbear/ance ....

forbid ....

forborne ....

force/ful ....

forcefully ....

forearm .... or ....

forecast ....

forecourt ....

forefinger ....

foregoing ....

foreground ....

foreign/er ....

foreman ....

foremost ....

forename ....

forensic ....

foresee/able ....

foreshadow ....

foresight ....

forest ....

foretell ....

forever .... or ....

foreword

forfeit/ure

forgery

forget/ful ... or

forgive/n

forgiveness ... or

forgot/ten ... or

fork

forlorn

form

formal

formality ... or

formally

format

formation

formative

former/ly

formidable

formula

forsake

fort

forth

forthcoming ... or

forthright

fortnight

fortress

fortuitous

fortunate

fortunately ... or

fortune

forty

forum

forward

foster

found

foundation

founder

fountain

four

fowl

fox

fracas

fraction

fracture

fragile

fragment/ation

fragmentary

fragrance

fragrant

frame

framework

franchise ... or

frank/ed

frankly

frantic/ally

fraud

fraudulent

fraught

fray

freak

free

freedom

freehold

freephone
freepost
freeze or
freezer
freight/er
French
frenzied
frequency
frequent/ly
fresh/en
fresheners
freshness
fretful or
friction
Friday or
fridge
friend/ship
frieze or
fright/en
frightful/ness
fringe or

frisky
fritter
frivolity or
frivolous
frog
from
front/age
frontier
frost/y
frown/ed
frozen
frugal
fruit/ful
fruitfulness
frustrate
frustration
fry
fuel
fugitive
fulfil
fulfillment

full/er
fullstop
fully
fumble
fume/s
fumigate
fun
function
functional or
fundamental
funds
funeral
funfair
fungus
funnel
funny
fur
furious
furnace
furnish
furniture

furore ....

furry ....

further/ance .... / ....

furthermore ....

furtive ....

fuse ....

fuselage ....

fuss/y .... / ....

futile ....

futility .... or ....

future ....

fuzzy ....

g

gaberdine

gable

gadget

gag

gain

gala

galactic

galaxy

gale

gallant

gallantry

galleon

gallery

gallon

gallop

gambit

gamble

game

gamekeeper or

gammon

gang

gangster

gangway

gap

garage

garb

garbage

garden/er

gargle

garland

garlic

garment

garnish

gas

gaseous

gasket

gastric

gate

gâteau

gather

gaudy

gauge

gaunt

gauze

gave

gay

gaze

gazette

gazetteer

gear

gearbox

geisha

gelignite

gender

genealogy

general

generalization

generalize

generally

generate

generation

generosity

generous

generously … or …

genes

genetics

genial

genius

genteel

gentile

gentle

gentleman … or …

gentlemen … or …

genuine

geographical

geography

geologist/geology

geometry

geranium

germ/s

German

germinate

gesticulate

gesture/s

get

ghastly

ghost

giant

giblets … or …

giddy

gift

gigantic

giggle

gimmick

ginger

gingerbread

gird/er

girl/ish

giro

Girobank

girth

gist

give/n

glacier

glad/ly

glade

glamour

glamorous

glance

gland

glare

glass/es

glaze

gleam

glib

glider

glimpse

glisten
glitter
gloat
global
gloom
glorious
gloss
glossary
glove
glow
glucose
glue
glutton/y
gnash
gnome
go
goal
goat
gobble/d
goblet
god
godsend
go-kart
gold/en
golf
gondola
good
good-bye
good-natured
goodness
goodnight
goodwill
gooseberry
gorge
gorgeous
gospel
gossip
gouge
goulash
gourmet
govern
government
grab ... or
grace/ful ... or
grade
gradient
gradual/ly
graduate/d
graffiti
graft
grain
gram ... or ... (e)
grammar
grammatical
gramophone
grand
grandchild ... or
granddaughter ... or
grandfather ... or
grandmother ... or
grandparents ... or
grandson ... or
grandstand ... or

grant
granule
grapefruit
graph ... or ... (e)
graphics ... or
graphite ... or
graphologist ... or
graphology ... or
grapple
grasp ... or
grass ... or
grate
grateful ... or
gratify
gratitude
gratuitous
gratuity
grave
gravity ... or
graze
great/er ... /

greatest
greed/ily ... /
greedy
Greek ... or
green
greengrocer ... or
greenhouse
gregarious
grew
grey
grid
grief
grievance
grieve
grievous
grill ... or
grim/e
grimace
grip
grizzle
grocer ... or

groceries ... or
grocery ... or
groom
groove
gross/ly ... /
grotesque
grotto
ground/less ... /
group
grouse
grovel
grow
growl
grown
growth
grudge
gruesome
gruff/ly ... /
grumble
guarantee
guarantor

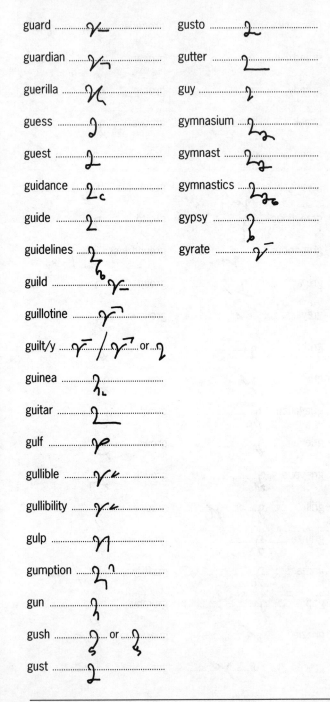

guard ....

guardian ....

guerilla ....

guess ....

guest ....

guidance ....

guide ....

guidelines ....

guild ....

guillotine ....

guilt/y .... / .... or ....

guinea ....

guitar ....

gulf ....

gullible ....

gullibility ....

gulp ....

gumption ....

gun ....

gush .... or ....

gust ....

gusto ....

gutter ....

guy ....

gymnasium ....

gymnast ....

gymnastics ....

gypsy ....

gyrate ....

haberdashery
habit/able
habitation
habitual
hackneyed
hacksaw
had
haddock
haggard
haggle
hail
hair
hairdresser

hake
half
half-hearted
hall
hallmark
hallucinate
hallucination
halo
halt
ham
hamburger
hamfisted
hammer
hammock
hamper
hand
handbag … or …
handbook … or …
handicap … or …
handicraft … or …
handkerchief … or …

handle
handsome … or …
handwriting … or …
handy/man
hang
hangover
hank
haphazard
happen
happily
happiness
happy
harass/ment
harbour
hard/ly … or …
hardship
hardware
hardwood
hardy
hare
hare-brained

harlequin
harm
harmful ... or ...
harmless
harmonious
harmony
harness
harrowing
harsh/ness
harvest
has
haste
hasty
hat
hatch
hate
hatred
haughty
haulage
haulier
haunt

have
haven
haversack
having
havoc
hay
hayfever
haystack
haywire
hazard
haze
hazel
hazy
he
head
headache
headlight
headlines
headlong
headquarters ... or
headset

headstrong
headway
health
healthiest
healthy
hear
heard
hearsay
heart/y
hearth
heartless
heart-rending
heat/ing
heath
heather ... or
Heathrow
heatstroke
heatwave
heaven/ly
heavily
heavy

hectic
hedge
hedgehog ... or ...
heedless
hefty
height
heir
heiress
heirloom
held
helicopter
helium
hello
helm
helmet
help/ful
helpless
hemisphere
hen
hence
henceforth ... or ...

her
herald
herb
herbaceous
here
hereafter
heredity
herewith
heritage
hermetic/ally
hermit
hero
heroine
herself
hesitate
hesitation
hexagon
hibernate
hibernation
hid/den
hideous

hierarchy
hierarchical
hi-fi
high/er
highlight
highness
high-rise
high speed
highway
hijack
hilarious
hilarity
hill
him
himself
hinder
hindrance
hinge ... or ...
hint/s
hire
hire-purchase ... or ...

his

historic/al

history

hit

hitch

hi-tech

hitherto

hoard

hoarse

hoax or

hobble

hobby

hockey

hod

hold

hole

holiday

hollow

holocaust

holster

homage

home/less

home-buyers

homely or

home-made

homeopathic

homeopathy

homesick

homicide

homogeneous

homonym

homophone

homosexual

honest/ly or / or

honey

honeymoon

honeysuckle

honorary or

honour/ed or /

honourable or

hood

hook

hooligan

hoop

Hoover

hop

hope

hopeful/ly /

hopeless/ness /

horizon

horizontal

hormone

horn

horoscope

horrendous

horrible

horribly

horror

horse

horse-drawn

horsepower

horseshoe

horticulture

hose

hospice ... or ...

hospitable ... or ...

hospital ... , ... or ...

hospitality ... , ... or ...

host

hostage

hostess

hostile

hostility ... or ...

hot

hotdog

hotel

hothead

hotplate

hotter

hour ... or ...

house

housebound

housebreaking

household

housekeeper ... or ...

housekeeping ... or ...

housewife

hovercraft

how

however ... or ...

howl

hug

huge

human

humane

humanitarian

humanity

humble/ness ... / ...

humbug ... or ...

humidity

humiliate

humiliation

humility ... or ...

humorous

humour

hundred ... or ... (g)

hung

hunger

hungrily

hungry

hunt/er ... / ...

hurdle

hurricane

hurry

hurt

hurtful ... or ...

husband ... or ...

hush

husk

hustle

hutch

hyacinth

hybrid

hydraulic

hydrofoil ... or ...

hydrogen

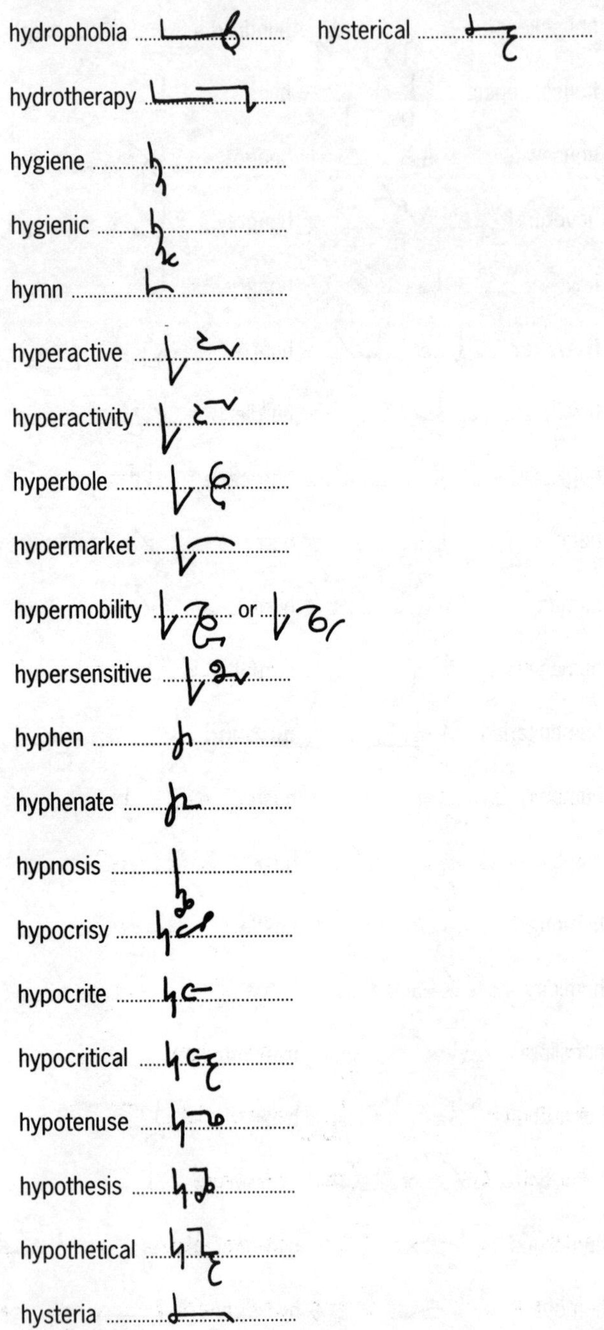
hydrophobia
hydrotherapy
hygiene
hygienic
hymn
hyperactive
hyperactivity
hyperbole
hypermarket
hypermobility
or
hypersensitive
hyphen
hyphenate
hypnosis
hypocrisy
hypocrite
hypocritical
hypotenuse
hypothesis
hypothetical
hysteria
hysterical

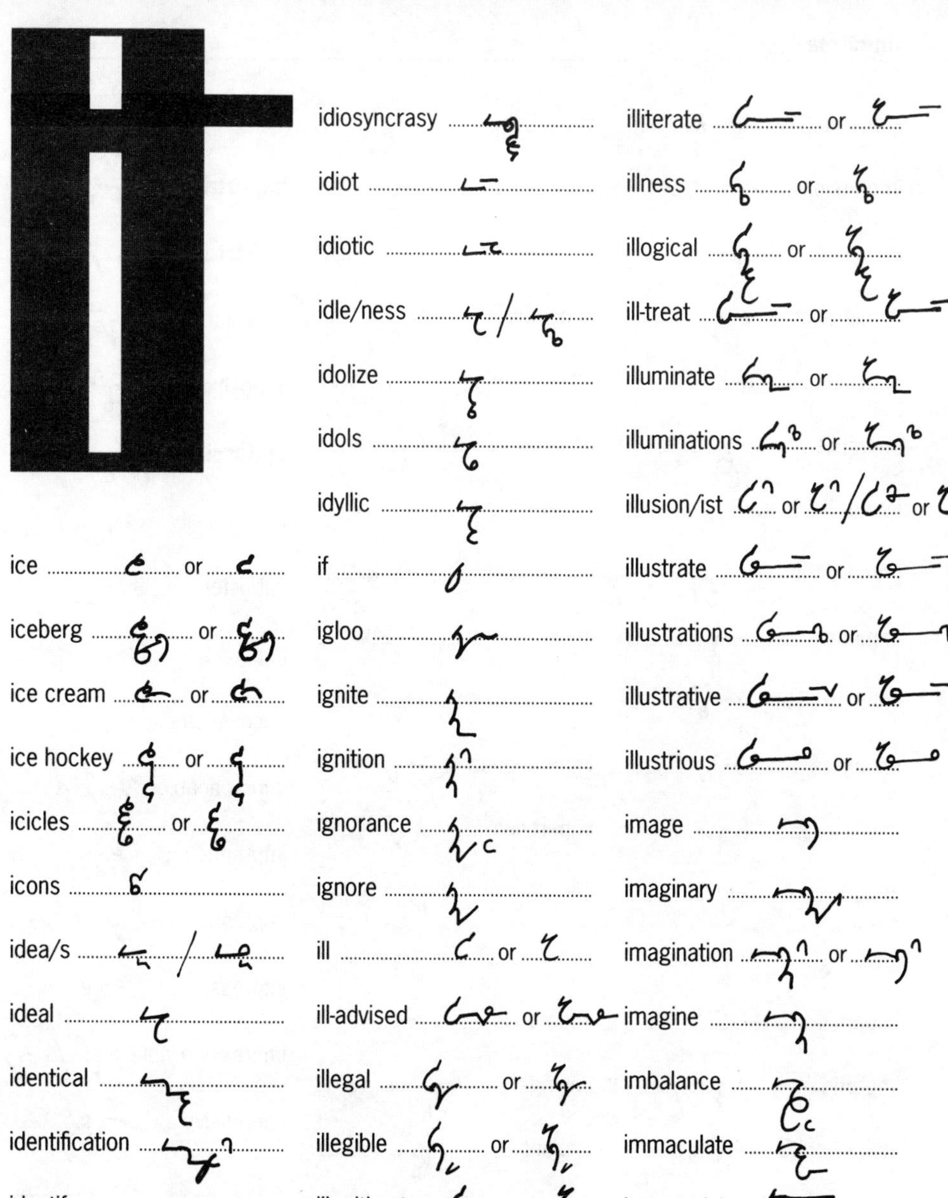

ice ... or ...

iceberg ... or ...

ice cream ... or ...

ice hockey ... or ...

icicles ... or ...

icons ...

idea/s ... / ...

ideal ...

identical ...

identification ...

identify ...

identity ...

ideological ...

ideology ...

idiosyncrasy ...

idiot ...

idiotic ...

idle/ness ... / ...

idolize ...

idols ...

idyllic ...

if ...

igloo ...

ignite ...

ignition ...

ignorance ...

ignore ...

ill ... or ...

ill-advised ... or ...

illegal ... or ...

illegible ... or ...

illegitimate ... or ...

ill-fated ... or ...

illicit ... or ...

illiteracy ... or ...

illiterate ... or ...

illness ... or ...

illogical ... or ...

ill-treat ... or ...

illuminate ... or ...

illuminations ... or ...

illusion/ist ... or ... / ... or ...

illustrate ... or ...

illustrations ... or ...

illustrative ... or ...

illustrious ... or ...

image ...

imaginary ...

imagination ... or ...

imagine ...

imbalance ...

immaculate ...

immaterial ...

immature ...

immediate/ly ... / ...

immense/ly ... / ... or ...

immerse

immersion

immigrant

immigration

imminent

immobile

immoral

immortal/ity

immune

immunization

immunize

imp

impact

impair

impart

impartial/ity

impassioned

impassive

impatience ... or

impatient

impeach/ment

impeccable

impede

impediment

impending

imperative

imperial

impermeable

impersonal

impersonate

impersonation

impertinence

impertinent

imperturbable ... or

impervious

impetuous

impinge ... or

implant

implement/ation

implication

implore

imply

import

importance

important/ly

importer

imposition

impossible

impossibility

imposter

impound

impoverish

impracticable

impregnate

impresario ... or

impress

impression/able

impressive

imprint

imprison/ment

improbable/
improbably

impromptu

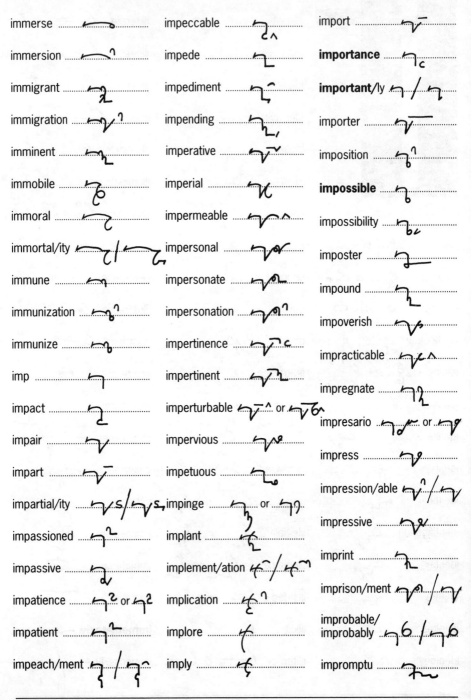

improper/ly .... / ....

improve/ment .... / ....

improvise ....

imprudent ....

impudent ....

impulse ....

impulsive ....

impure ....

in ....

inability ....

inaccessible .... or ....

inaccuracy .... or ....

inadequate ....

inadvertent/ly .... / ....

inapplicable ....

inappropriate .... or ....

inarticulate ....

inattention ....

inaudible ....

inaugural ....

inauguration ....

inborn ....

incalculable ....

incapable ....

incapacitate ....

incautious ....

incendiary ....

incense ....

incentive ....

inception ....

incessant ....

inch .... or ....

incidence ....

incident .... or ....

incidental .... or ....

incidentally .... or ....

incinerate ....

incision ....

inclement ....

inclination ....

incline ....

include ....

inclusive ....

incognito .... or ....

incoherent ....

income ....

income tax ....

incoming ....

incomparable ....

incompatible ....

incompetence ....

incompetent ....

incomplete ....

inconclusive ....

incongruous .... or ....

inconsiderate ....

inconsistency ....

inconsistent ....

inconsolable ....

inconspicuous ....

inconstancy ....

inconvenience ....

inconvenient ....

incorporated ... or ...
incorrect ...
incorrigible ...
increase ...
increasingly ...
incredible ...
incredulity ...
increment ...
incriminate ...
incubate ...
incumbent ...
incur/red ... / ...
incurable ...
indecent ... or ...
indebted ...
indeed ... or ...
indefatigable ...
indefensible ...
indefinite ...
indelible ...
indemnify ...

indemnity ...
indent ...
independence ...
independent/ly ... / ...
indescribable ...
indeterminate ...
index ... or ...
index-linked ...
indicate ...
indication ...
indices ...
indict/able ... / ...
indictment ...
indifferent ...
indignant/ly ... / ...
indignation ...
indiscriminate ...
indispensable ...
indisposed ...
individual ...
indoctrinate ...

indolence ...
indolent ...
indoors ...
induce/ment ... / ...
induct/ion ... / ...
indulge ...
industrial ...
industrialize ...
industrious ...
industry ... or ...(g)
inedible ...
inefficiency ... or ...
inefficient/ly ... / ...
ineligible ...
inept ...
inequality ...
inequitable ...
inertia ...
inestimable ...
inevitable ...
inexorable ...

inexpensive

inexperience

inexperienced

infallible

infamous

infant

infatuated

infect/ion

infer

inference

inferior

inferiority ... or ...

infest

infiltrate

infiltration

infinite

infinitive

infirm

inflame

inflammable

inflate

inflation

inflexible

inflict

influence

influential

influx

inform ... or ...

informal/ly ... or ... / ... or ...

information ... or ...

infrequent

infringe ... or ...

infuriate

ingenious

ingenuous

ingot

ingrained ... or ...

ingredients

inhabit

inhabitable

inhale

inherent

inherit

inhibit

inimitable

initial

initiate

initiation

initiative

inject/ion

injunction ... or ...

injure/s

injuries

injury

injustice

ink

inkling

inland

innate

innings

innocence ... or ...

innocent

innovate

innovation
innuendo
inoculate
inoculation
inoperable
inopportune
inordinate
input ...... or ......
inquest
inquire ...... or ......
inquiry
inquisition
inroad
insane
insatiable
inscribe
inscription
inscrutable
insect
insecure
insensible

insert/ed ...... or ......
inset ...... or ......
inside ...... or ......
insidious
insight
insignia
insignificance
insignificant
insincere
insinuate ...... or ......
insipid
insist
insistence
insistent
insolence
insomnia
inspect
inspection
inspector
inspiration
inspire

instability
install
installation
instalment
instance
instant/ly ...... or ......
instantaneous
instead
instigate
instil
instinct
instinctive/ly
institute
institution/al
instruct/ion
instructive
instructor
instrument/al
insubordinate
insubordination
insufficient

insulate
insulation
insuperable
insurance
insure/rs
intact ... or ...
intake ... or ...
intangible
integral
integrate
integration
integrity
intellect/ual
intelligence
intelligent
intelligible
intend ... or ...
intense ... or ...
intensive ... or ...
intent ... or ...
intention/al

interact/ion
interchange ... or ...
intercom
intercontinental
interest
interface
interfere
interference
interim
interior
interlock
intermediary
intimidate
intermission
intermittent
internal
international
Interpol
interpret
interpreter
interrogate

interrogation
interrupt/ion
intersperse
interstate
interval
intervene
intervention
interview
intestate
intimate
intimidate
intimidation
into
intolerance
intolerant
intrigue
intrinsic
introduce
introduction
introvert
intruder

intrusion .... or ....
intuition .... or ....
inundate ....
invalid ....
invaluable ....
invasion ....
invention ....
inventive ....
inventor/y ....
inverted ....
invest ....
investigate ....
investigation ....
investigator ....
investment ....
investors ....
invigilate ....
invigilator ....
invisible ....
invitation ....
invite ....

invoice ....
invoke ....
involve/ment ....
inward ....
irate ....
iridescent ....
iron ....
ironic ....
irony ....
irrational ....
irrecoverable ....
irrefutable ....
irregular/ity ....
irrelevant ....
irreparable/y ....
irresistable ....
irrespective ....
irresponsible ....
irretrievable ....
irrevocable ....
irrigate ....

irrigation ....
irritate ....
irritation ....
is ....
island .... or ....
isle .... or ....
isolate .... or ....
isolation .... or ....
isometric ....
isotope ....
issue ....
it ....
Italian ....
italics ....
itch ....
item ....
itemize ....
itinerary ....
itself ....
ivory ....
ivy ....

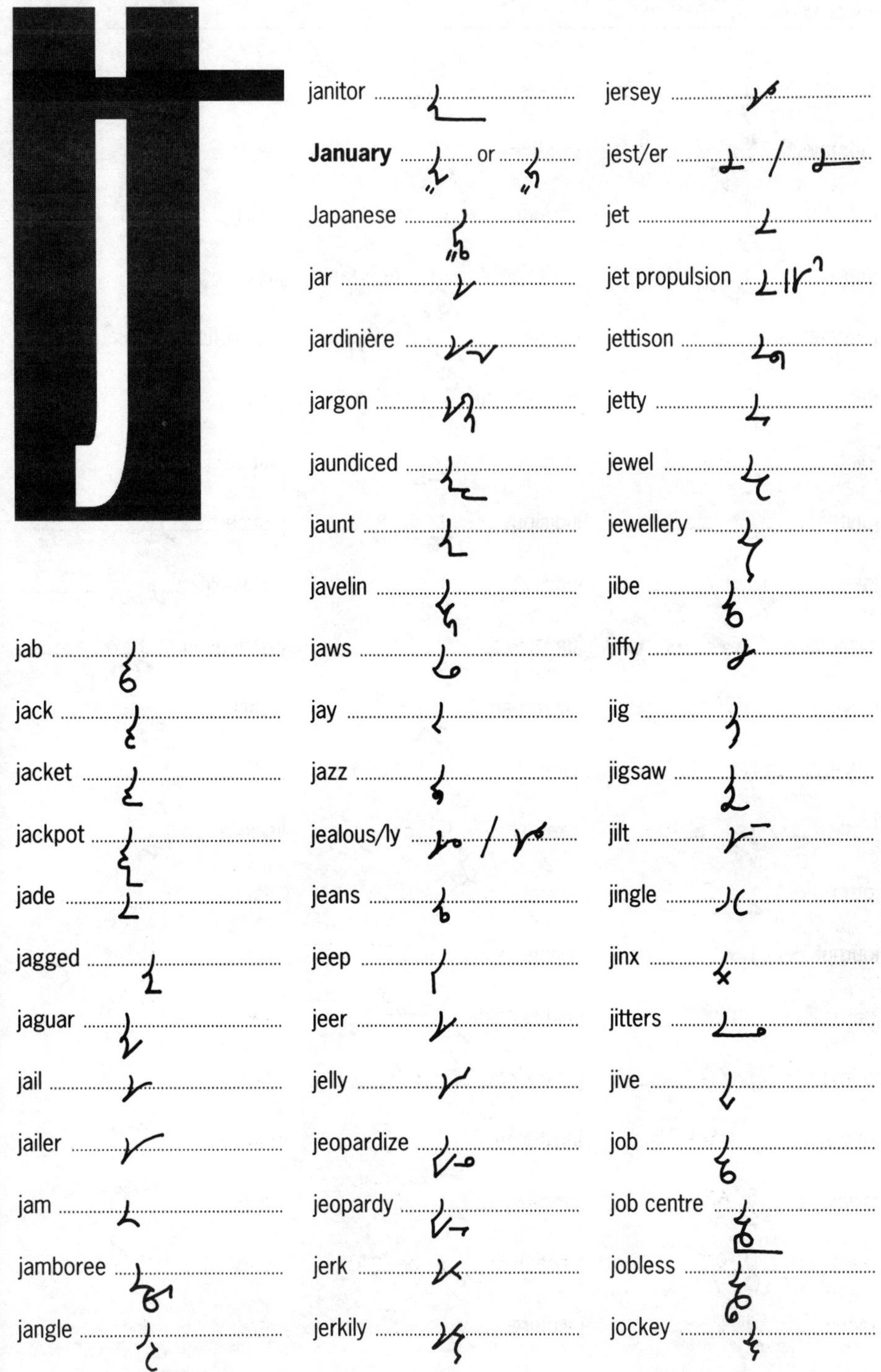

J

jab

jack

jacket

jackpot

jade

jagged

jaguar

jail

jailer

jam

jamboree

jangle

janitor

January or

Japanese

jar

jardinière

jargon

jaundiced

jaunt

javelin

jaws

jay

jazz

jealous/ly /

jeans

jeep

jeer

jelly

jeopardize

jeopardy

jerk

jerkily

jersey

jest/er /

jet

jet propulsion

jettison

jetty

jewel

jewellery

jibe

jiffy

jig

jigsaw

jilt

jingle

jinx

jitters

jive

job

job centre

jobless

jockey

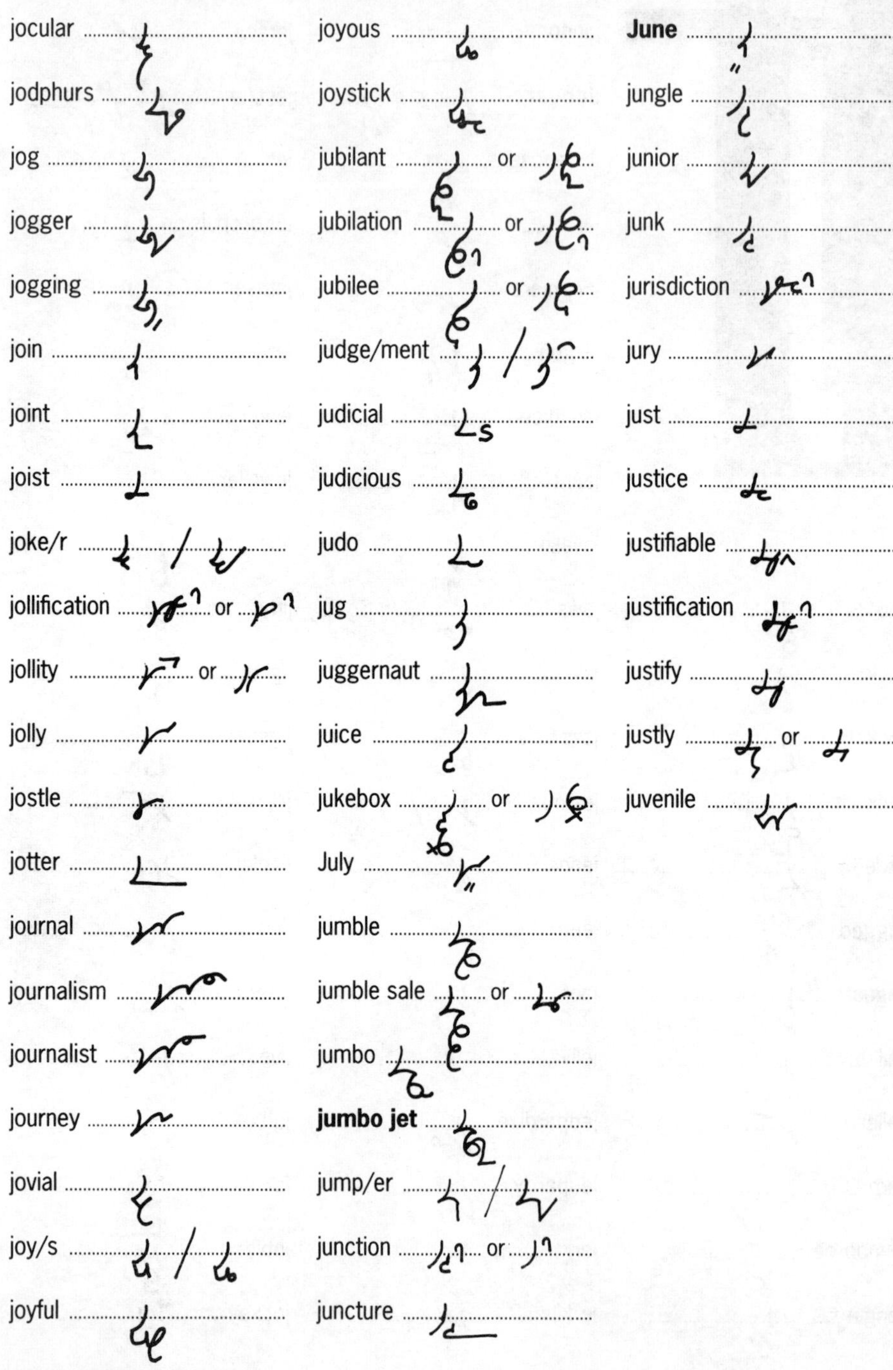

jocular
jodphurs
jog
jogger
jogging
join
joint
joist
joke/r
jollification ... or ...
jollity ... or ...
jolly
jostle
jotter
journal
journalism
journalist
journey
jovial
joy/s
joyful

joyous
joystick
jubilant ... or ...
jubilation ... or ...
jubilee ... or ...
judge/ment
judicial
judicious
judo
jug
juggernaut
juice
jukebox ... or ...
July
jumble
jumble sale ... or ...
jumbo
jumbo jet
jump/er
junction ... or ...
juncture

June
jungle
junior
junk
jurisdiction
jury
just
justice
justifiable
justification
justify
justly ... or ...
juvenile

kaftan

kale

kaleidoscope

kangaroo

karate

kayak

kebab

kedgeree

keel

keel over

keen/ness

keep/er

keepsake

keg

kennel

kept

kerb

kernel

kerosene

kestrel

ketch

ketchup

kettle

key

keyboard

kibbutz

kick

kid

kidnap/per

kidney

kill

kiln

kilobyte

kilogram

kilometre or

kilt

kimono

kin

kind/est

kindergarten or

kindle

kindliness

kindly or

kindness

kindred

kinetic

king

kingdom

kingliness

kingly

kingship

kinship

kiosk

kiss/es

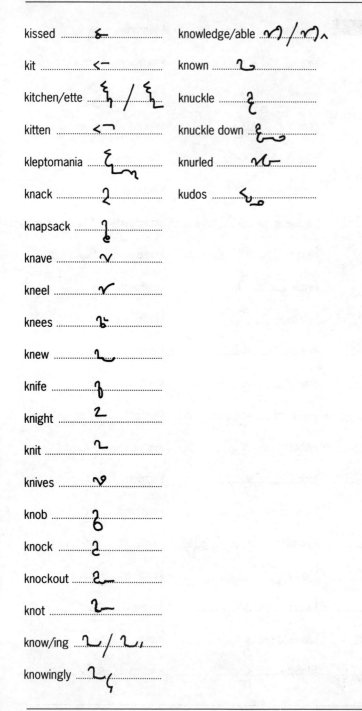

kissed ....

kit ....

kitchen/ette ....

kitten ....

kleptomania ....

knack ....

knapsack ....

knave ....

kneel ....

knees ....

knew ....

knife ....

knight ....

knit ....

knives ....

knob ....

knock ....

knockout ....

knot ....

know/ing ....

knowingly ....

knowledge/able ....

known ....

knuckle ....

knuckle down ....

knurled ....

kudos ....

L

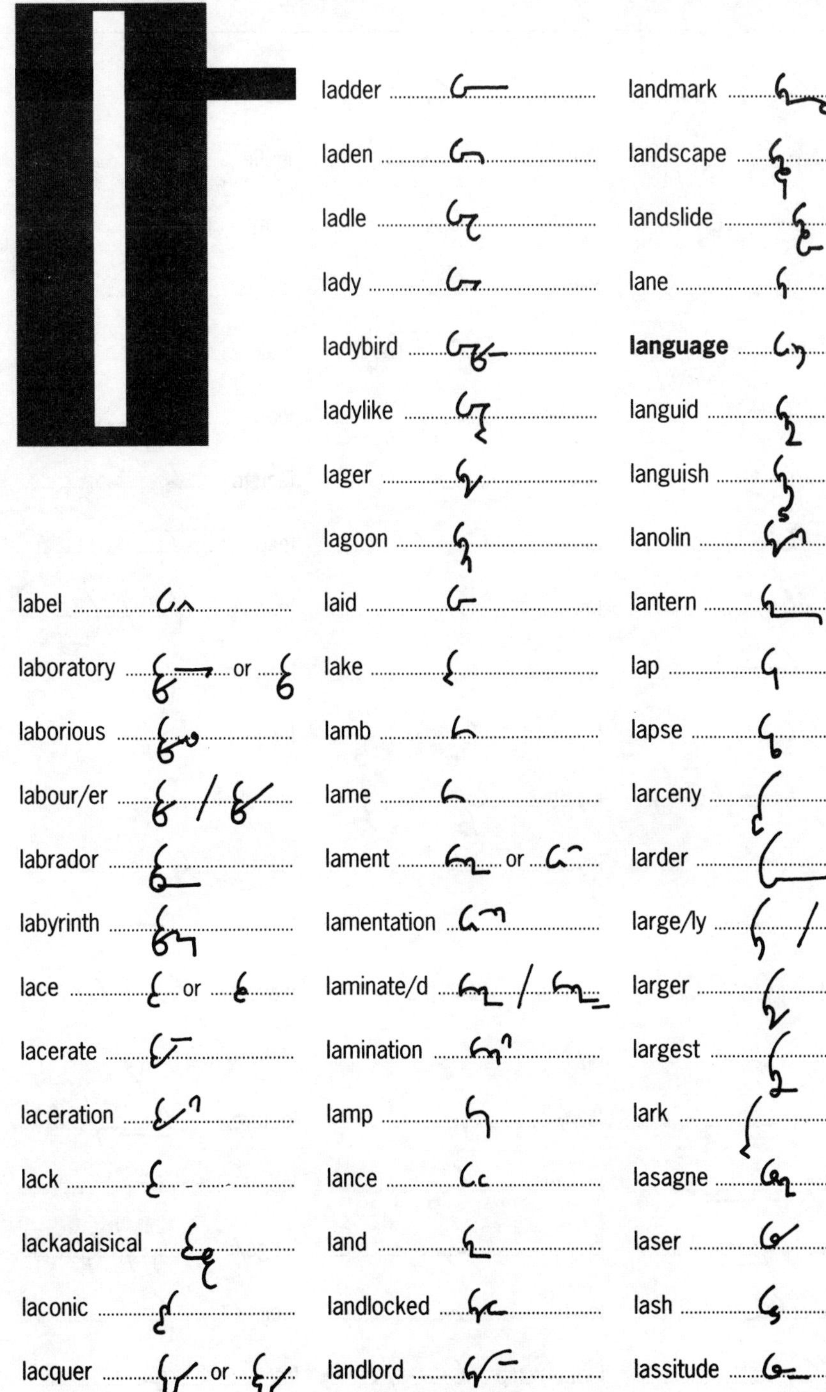

label
laboratory ... or ...
laborious
labour/er
labrador
labyrinth
lace ... or ...
lacerate
laceration
lack
lackadaisical
laconic
lacquer ... or ...

ladder
laden
ladle
lady
ladybird
ladylike
lager
lagoon
laid
lake
lamb
lame
lament ... or ...
lamentation
laminate/d
lamination
lamp
lance
land
landlocked
landlord

landmark
landscape
landslide
lane
language
languid
languish
lanolin
lantern
lap
lapse
larceny
larder
large/ly
larger
largest
lark
lasagne
laser
lash
lassitude

last/ly
latch
late/ly
latent
later
lateral
latest
latex
lathe
lather
latitude
latter/ly
lattice
laudable
laugh/able
laughter
launch
launderette
laundry
laurel ... or
lava

lavatory
lavender
lavish
law
lawful/ly
lawless
lawn
lawyer
lax
lay
layabout ... or
lay-by ... or
layers
layette
layman
lay-off
lazily
laziness
lazy
lead
leader/ship

leaf
leaflet
leafy
league
leak
lean
lean-to
leap
learn/ed
learner
lease
leasehold
least ... or
leather
leave/r
lecherous
lecture/r
led
ledge/r
leer
left

left-handed
leg
legacy
legal
legality ... or ...
legalization
legally
legation
legend/ary
leggings
legible
legion
legislation
legislative
legislator
legitimate/ly ... / ...
legitimize
legless
leisure
lemon
lemonade

lend
length/en ... / ...
lengthy
leniency
lenient
leotard
less/en ... or ...
lessee
lesson ... or ...
lessor
let
lethal
lethargic
lethargy
letter/s ... / ...
lettuce
level
level-headed
lever
leverage
levitation

levity
liability
liable
liaise
liaison
libel
libellous
liberal/ly ... / ...
liberality ... or ...
liberate
liberation
liberty
library ... or ...
licence ... or ...
licensee ... or ...
licenser ... or ...
licentiate
licentious
lick
lido
lie

lieutenant
life ... or
lifeboat
lifeless ... or
lifelines ... or
lifelong ... or
lifespan ... or
lifestyle ... or
lifetime
lift
ligament
light
light-coloured
lighter
light-hearted
lighthouse
lightness
lightning
lightweight
like/able
likelihood
likely
likeness
likewise
lilac
limb/less
limber
lime
limelight
limerick
limit/ed
limousine
linctus ... or
line
lineage
linear
linen
liner
lingerie ... or
linguist/ic
liniment
lining
link/age
linoleum
lintel
lion
lip
lip-read
lipstick
liquid/ate
liquidation
liquidator
liquidize/r
liquorice
lisp
list
listen/er
listless
literal/ly
literacy
literate
literature
lithe

lithography
litigation
litmus
litre
litter
little
live
livelihood
liveliness
lively
liven
liver
livestock
load
loaf ... or ...
loan
loath/e
loathsome
lobby
lobe
lobster

local/ly ... / ...
locality ... or ...
localize
locate
location
lock/er ... / ...
locket
lockout
locomotion
locomotive
lodge
loft
loftiness
logbook
logarithm
loggerheads
logic
logical
logistics
logo
loin

loiter
lollipop ... or ...
loneliness
lonely
lonesome
long
long-distance
longer
longevity
longhand
longing/ly ... / ...
longitude
long-range ... or ...
long-term
long-time ... or ...
long-winded
look/ed ... / ...
lookout
loom
loophole
loose/n ... / ...

loquacious ....

lorry ....

lose/r .... / ....

loss ....

lost ....

lot ....

lotion ....

lottery ....

loud ....

loudspeaker ....

lounge .... or ....

louse .... or ....

lovable ....

love ....

lovely ....

loving/ly .... / ....

low/er .... / ....

lowly ....

loyal/ly ....

loyalty ....

lozenge .... or ....

Ltd. ....

lubricate .... or ....

lubrication ....

lucid/ity .... / ....

luck/ily .... / ....

lucky ....

lucrative .... or ....

ludicrous ....

luggage ....

lukewarm ....

lumbago .... or ....

lumber ....

lumberjack .... or ....

luminous ....

lump ....

lunar ....

lunatic ....

lunch ....

luncheon ....

lunchtime ....

lung ....

lurid .... or ....

luscious ....

lush ....

lustre ....

lustrous ....

luxuriant ....

luxuries ....

luxurious/ly .... / ....

luxury ....

lymph ....

lynch ....

lyric ....

lyrical ....

macabre

macadam

macaroon

machete

machine

machinery

machinist

mackintosh

mad/made

madam

maestro

magazine

magic/al

magician

magistrate or (g)

magnanimity

magnanimous

magnate or

magnesium or

magnet or

magnetic or

magnetism or

magnetize or

magneto or

magnificence

magnificent

magnify

magnitude or

magnolia or

magnum

magpie

mahogany

maid

mail

main

mainframe

mainly or

mainstay

maintain

maintenance

maisonette

maize/maze or

majestically

majesty

major

majority or

make/r

make-belief

make-believe

makeshift

maladjusted

malaise

malapropism

male

malformation

malfunction or
malice
malicious
malign
malignancy
mallet
malnutrition
malpractice
mammal
mammoth
man
manacle
manage
manager/ess
managerial
management
mandate
manger
mangle
manhole
maniac

manicure
manifest/ation
manifold
manilla
manipulate
manipulation
mankind
man-made
mannequin
manner
manoeuvre
manor
manpower
mansion
manslaughter
mantelpiece or
manual
manufacture/r
manuscript
many
map

mar
marathon
marble
March or
margarine
margin/al
marina
marine
maritime
mark/et
marketable
marketing
marksman
marmalade
marquee
marrow
marriage
marry
marshall
martial
martyr

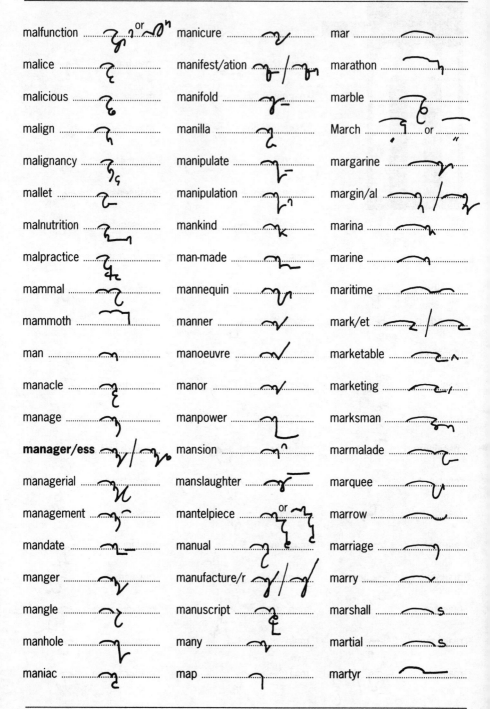

marvel
marvellous
marzipan
mascara or
mascot or
masculine or
mash
masochism or
masochist or
mason
mass
massacre or
massage
masseur
massive
master/ly
masterful or
mastermind
masterpiece or
mastiff
mat

match/less
matchbox
matchwood
mate
material
materialism
materialistic
maternal
maths
mathematician
mathematics
matinée
matriarch
matriculate
matrimony
matrix
matter
mattress
mature
maxim
maximum

may
mayhem
mayonnaise
mayor
mayoress
me
meadow
meagre
meal
mean
meander
meaningful
meant
meantime
meanwhile or
measure/ment
meat
mechanic
mechanical
mechanism
mechanization

medal
medallion
media
mediaeval
medical
medicine
mediocre
meditation
meditate
Mediterranean ... or
medium
meek/ness
meet
megabyte
megalomania
megaphone
megaton
melancholy
melodrama
melody
melon

melt
member
membership
memento
memo
memoirs
memorandum
memorial
memories
memorize
memory
men
menace
menagerie
mend
menial
mental/ity ... or
mention
mentor
menu/s
mercantile

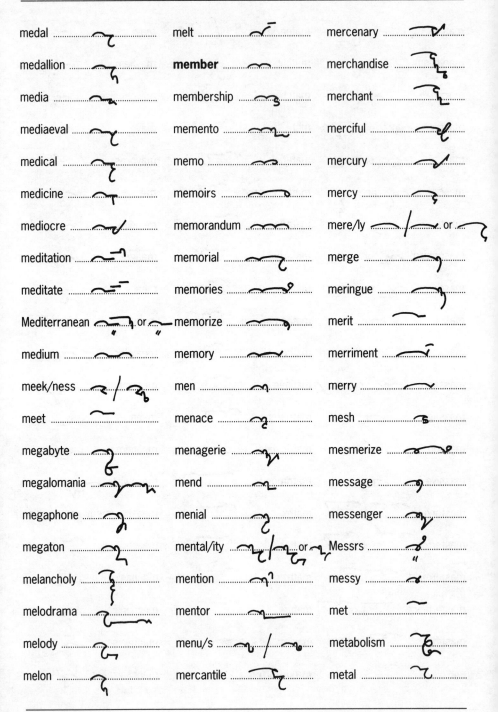

mercenary
merchandise
merchant
merciful
mercury
mercy
mere/ly ... or
merge
meringue
merit
merriment
merry
mesh
mesmerize
message
messenger
Messrs
messy
met
metabolism
metal

metallurgy or
metamorphosis
metaphor
meteor/ic
meteorological
meteorologist
meteorology
meter
methane
method/ical
meticulous
metre
metric/ation
metro
metronome
metropolitan or
Mexican
mezzanine
mice
microbe or
microbiology

microchip
microcomputer
micro-electronics
microfiche
microfilm
micron
microphone
microprocessing
microprocessor
microscope
microwave
midday
middle
middle-aged
midget
midnight
midsummer
midway
midwife
might
migraine

migrate
mile/age
milestone
militant or
military or
milk/man
millstone
millennium
milligram
millilitre or
millimetre
million or (g)
mince/meat
mind/less
mine/r
minestrone
mingle
miniature
minibus
minicomputer
minimize

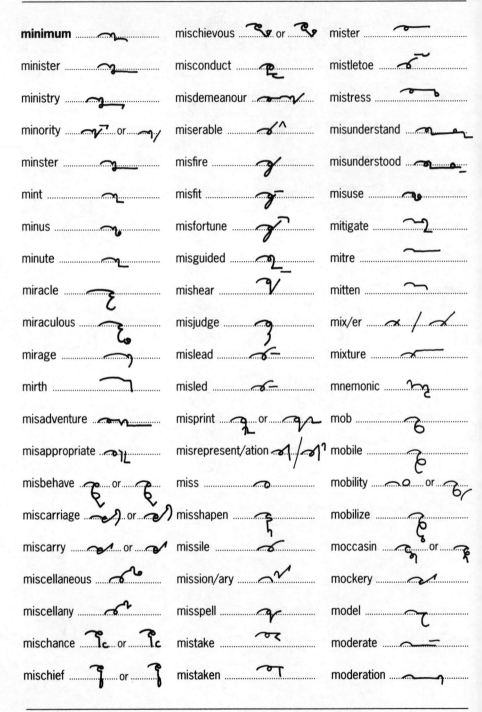

minimum
minister
ministry
minority ... or ...
minster
mint
minus
minute
miracle
miraculous
mirage
mirth
misadventure
misappropriate
misbehave ... or ...
miscarriage ... or ...
miscarry ... or ...
miscellaneous
miscellany
mischance ... or ...
mischief ... or ...
mischievous ... or ...
misconduct
misdemeanour
miserable
misfire
misfit
misfortune
misguided
mishear
misjudge
mislead
misled
misprint ... or ...
misrepresent/ation
miss
misshapen
missile
mission/ary
misspell
mistake
mistaken
mister
mistletoe
mistress
misunderstand
misunderstood
misuse
mitigate
mitre
mitten
mix/er
mixture
mnemonic
mob
mobile
mobility ... or ...
mobilize
moccasin ... or ...
mockery
model
moderate
moderation

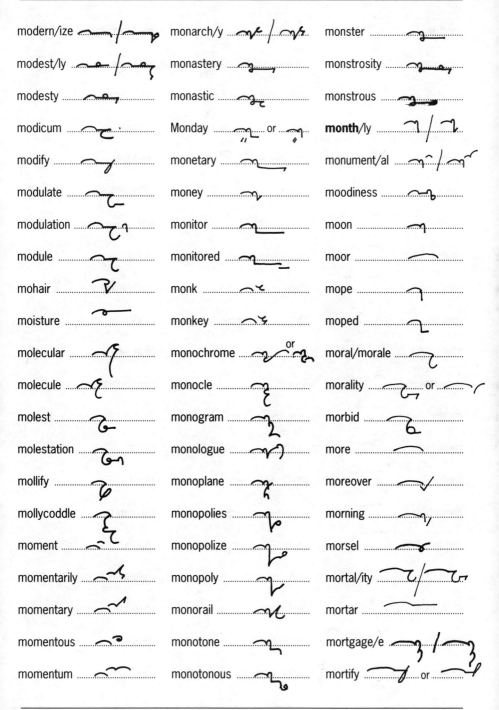

modern/ize
modest/ly
modesty
modicum
modify
modulate
modulation
module
mohair
moisture
molecular
molecule
molest
molestation
mollify
mollycoddle
moment
momentarily
momentary
momentous
momentum

monarch/y
monastery
monastic
Monday or
monetary
money
monitor
monitored
monk
monkey
monochrome or
monocle
monogram
monologue
monoplane
monopolies
monopolize
monopoly
monorail
monotone
monotonous

monster
monstrosity
monstrous
month/ly
monument/al
moodiness
moon
moor
mope
moped
moral/morale
morality or
morbid
more
moreover
morning
morsel
mortal/ity
mortar
mortgage/e
mortify or

mortuary
mosaic
most
motel
moth
moth-eaten
mother/ly
motherhood
mother-in-law
motion
motionless
motivate
motive
motivation
motor
motorbike
motorcycle
motorist
motorway
mottled
motto

mould
mountain/eer
mourn/ful
mouse
moustache
mouth
mouthpiece
move/ment
mow
Mr
Mrs
much
mud/dy
muddle
muffle
mug
mule
mull
multi-coloured
multifarious
multi-lateral

multi-millionaire
multiple
multiplication
multiplicity
multiply
multi-racial
multi-storey
multitude
multitudinous
munch
mundane
municipal
municipality ... or ...
mural
murder
murderer
murmur
muscle
muscular ... or ...
museum
mushroom

music/al .... / ....

musician ....

must ....

mustard ....

mutilate ....

mutilation ....

mutton ....

mutual/ly .... / ....

muzzle ....

my ....

myself ....

mysterious ....

mystic/al .... / ....

mystified .... or ....

mystify .... or ....

mystique ....

myth ....

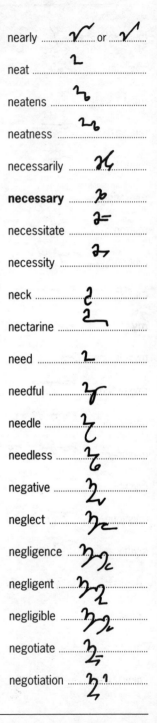

nail ....

naïve ....

name ....

nameless ....

namely .... or ....

nape ....

narrate ....

narrow ....

narrowly ....

nation .... or .... (b)

national ....

nationalism ....

nationalization ....

nationalize ....

nationality ....

nationwide ....

natives ....

natural ....

naturally ....

naturalist ....

nature ....

naturopath ....

naturopathic ....

naturopathy ....

naughty ....

nautical ....

naval/navel ....

nave ....

navigable ....

navigate ....

navigation ....

navigator ....

near ....

nearby ....

nearly .... or ....

neat ....

neatens ....

neatness ....

necessarily ....

necessary ....

necessitate ....

necessity ....

neck ....

nectarine ....

need ....

needful ....

needle ....

needless ....

negative ....

neglect ....

negligence ....

negligent ....

negligible ....

negotiate ....

negotiation ....

neighbour
neighbourhood
neighbouring
neighbourly
neither
nephew
nerves
nervous
nest
nestle
net
nether
network
neutral
neutralize
neutron
never ... or ...
nevertheless ... or ...
new
newly
newsagent ... or ...

newspaper
newt
New York
next ... or ...
nib
nibble
nice ... or ...
nicely ... or ...
niche
nickel
nickname
nicotine
niece ... or ...
niggardly ... or ...
nigh
night
nightly ... or ...
nightmare
nimble
nine
ninth

nip
nipple
nitrate
nitrous
no
nobble ... or ...
noble/nobly ... or ...
nobility
nocturnal
nocturne
nod
nodule
noise
noisily
noisy
nomad
nominal
nominate
nomination
nonchalant
nonconformist ... or ...

nonconformity ... or ...
nondescript ...
none ... or ...
nonentity ...
nonsense ...
non-stop ...
noodle ...
nook ...
noon ... or ...
no one ...
noose ...
nor ...
Nordic ...
Norfolk ...
normal ... or ...
normality ... or ...
normally ... or ...
Norse ...
north/northern ...
Norwegian ...
nose ...

nostalgia ...
nostalgic ...
nostril ...
nosy ...
not ...
notable ...
notary ...
notation ...
notch ...
note ...
notebook ...
nothing ...
notice ... or ...
noticeable ... or ...
notifiable ...
notification ...
notify ...
notion ...
notional ...
notorious ...
notwithstanding ...

nought ...
noun ...
nourish ...
nourishment ...
novel ...
novelist ...
novelty ...
November ...
novice ...
now ...
nowadays ...
nowhere ... or ...
noxious ...
nozzle ...
nuance ...
nuclear ...
nucleus ...
nudge ...
nuisance ...
null ...
nullify ...

numb ....

number .... or ....

numerable ....

numeral ....

numerate ....

numerator ....

numeric ....

numerical ....

numerology ....

numerous ....

numismatic ....

nun ....

nunnery ....

nuptial ....

nurse ....

nursery ....

nurture ....

nut ....

nutmeg ....

nutria ....

nutrient ....

nutrition ....

nutritional ....

nutritious ....

nutritive ....

nutshell ....

nutty ....

nylon ....

nymph ....

oaf

oak

oar or

oasis

oast

oats

oath

obdurate

obedience

obedient

obeisance

obelisk

obese

obey

obituary

object

objection

objectionable

objective

obligate

obligation

obligatory

oblige

oblique

obliterate

oblivion

oblivious

oblong

obnoxious

oboe

obscene

obscure

obsequious

observance

observant

observation

observe

obsess

obsessed

obsolescent

obsolete

obstacle

obstinate

obstreperous

obstruct

obstruction

obstructive

obtain/obtainable

obtained

obtuse

obvious

obviously

occasion

occasional/ly

occult

occupant
occupation
occupier
occupy
occur
occurrence
ocean
oceanic
o'clock or
octagon
octane
octant
octave
October
ocular
oculist
odd
oddity
oddments
odious
odium

odorous
odour
odyssey
of
off
offence or
offend or
offender or
offensive or
offer
offhand
office or
officer or
official or
officially or
officiate or
officious or
offset
offshore or
offspring
oft

often or
ogle
oh
oil
ointment
old
older
oldest
old-established
old-fashioned
olive
Olympian
Olympics
ombudsman
omelette
omen
ominous
omission
omit
omnibus
omnipotent

omnipotence
on/one
once
oneself or
onion
onlooker
only
onset
onshore
onslaught
onto
onus
onward
onyx
opal
opaline
opaque
open
open-handed
opening
openly

opera
operate
operatic
operation
operative
operator
opiate
opinion
opium
opponent
opportune
opportunism
opportunity
oppose
opposed
opposite
opposition
oppress
opt
optic
optical

optician
optimism
optimist
optimistic
optimistically
option
optional
opulent
opus
or
oracle
oral
orange
orate
oration
orator
oratorio
oratory
orb
orbit
orchard

orchestra
orchestral
orchestrate
orchestration
orchid
ordain
ordeal
order
orderly
ordinal
ordinance
ordinarily
ordinary
ordination
ordnance
ore
organ
organism
organist
organization
organize

orgy
oriel
orient
oriental
orientate
orienteering
orifice
origin
original
originally
originate
oriole
ormolu
ornament
ornamental
ornamentation
ornate
orphan
orphanage
orrery
orthodox

oscillate ... or ...
osmosis
osprey
ossicle
ossify ... or ...
ostensible
ostentation
osteopath
osteopathy
ostracize
ostrich
other
otherwise
otter
ottoman
ought
ounce
our
ourselves
oust
out

outback ....
outbreak ....
outcome ....
outcry ....
outdoors ....
outer ....
outfit ....
outing ....
outlaw ....
outlay ....
outline ....
outlook ....
outlying ....
outnumber .... or ....
output ....
outrage ....
outrageous ....
outright ....
outset ....
outside ....
outskirts ....

outstanding ....
outwardly ....
outwards ....
oval ....
ovary ....
ovation ....
oven ....
over .... or ....(b)(e)
overbalance ....
overbearing ....
overboard ....
overcame ....
overcoat ....
overcome ....
overcrowded ....
overdose ....
overdraft ....
overdrive ....
overdue ....
overfed ....
overflow ....

overgrown ....
overheard ....
overlap ....
overload ....
overlook ....
overnight ....
overpower/ed .... / ....
overpowering ....
overprinting ....
override ....
overrule ....
overrun ....
overseas ....
oversee ....
overseer ....
overshoes ....
overtake/n .... / ....
overtime ....
overtook ....
overtype ....
overweight ....

overwhelm ....

owe ....

owing ....

owl ....

own ....

owned ....

owner ....

ox ....

oxen ....

oxide ....

oxidize ....

oxygen ....

oxygenate ....

oyster ....

ozone ....

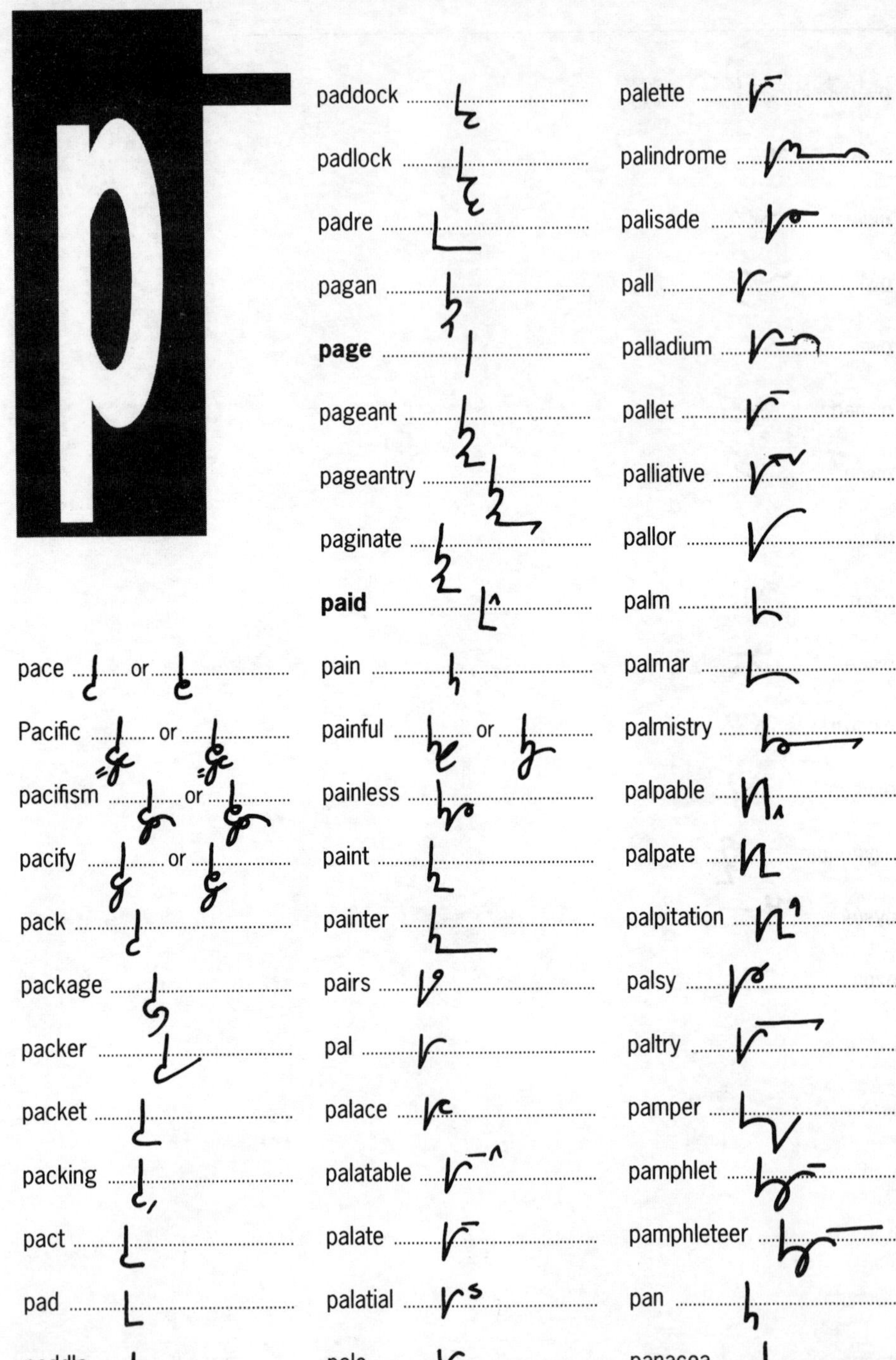

p

pace ... or ...

Pacific ... or ...

pacifism ... or ...

pacify ... or ...

pack

package

packer

packet

packing

pact

pad

paddle

paddock

padlock

padre

pagan

page

pageant

pageantry

paginate

paid

pain

painful ... or ...

painless

paint

painter

pairs

pal

palace

palatable

palate

palatial

pale

palette

palindrome

palisade

pall

palladium

pallet

palliative

pallor

palm

palmar

palmistry

palpable

palpate

palpitation

palsy

paltry

pamper

pamphlet

pamphleteer

pan

panacea

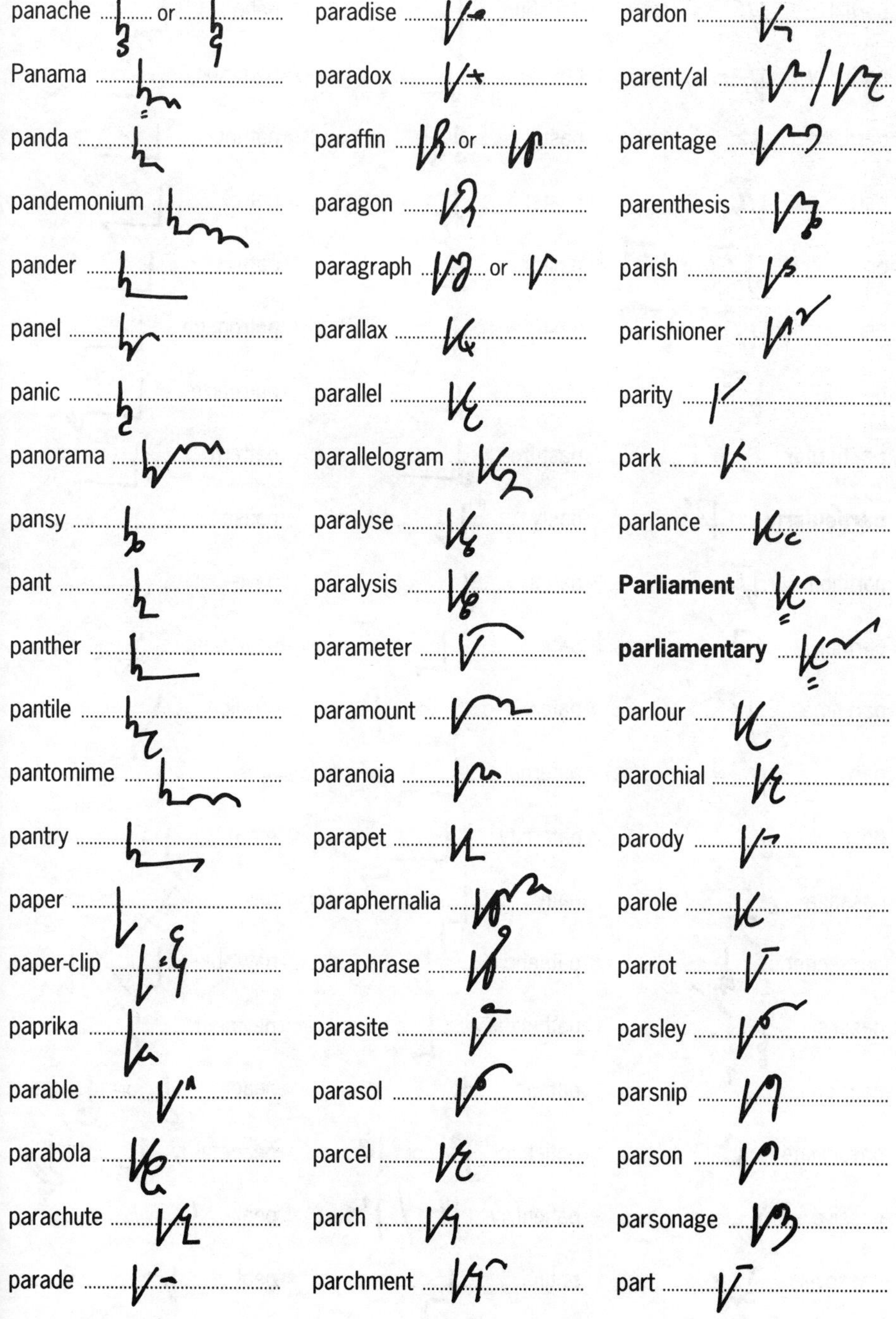

panache ...... or ......
Panama ......
panda ......
pandemonium ......
pander ......
panel ......
panic ......
panorama ......
pansy ......
pant ......
panther ......
pantile ......
pantomime ......
pantry ......
paper ......
paper-clip ......
paprika ......
parable ......
parabola ......
parachute ......
parade ......
paradise ......
paradox ......
paraffin ...... or ......
paragon ......
paragraph ...... or ......
parallax ......
parallel ......
parallelogram ......
paralyse ......
paralysis ......
parameter ......
paramount ......
paranoia ......
parapet ......
paraphernalia ......
paraphrase ......
parasite ......
parasol ......
parcel ......
parch ......
parchment ......
pardon ......
parent/al ......
parentage ......
parenthesis ......
parish ......
parishioner ......
parity ......
park ......
parlance ......
Parliament ......
parliamentary ......
parlour ......
parochial ......
parody ......
parole ......
parrot ......
parsley ......
parsnip ......
parson ......
parsonage ......
part ......

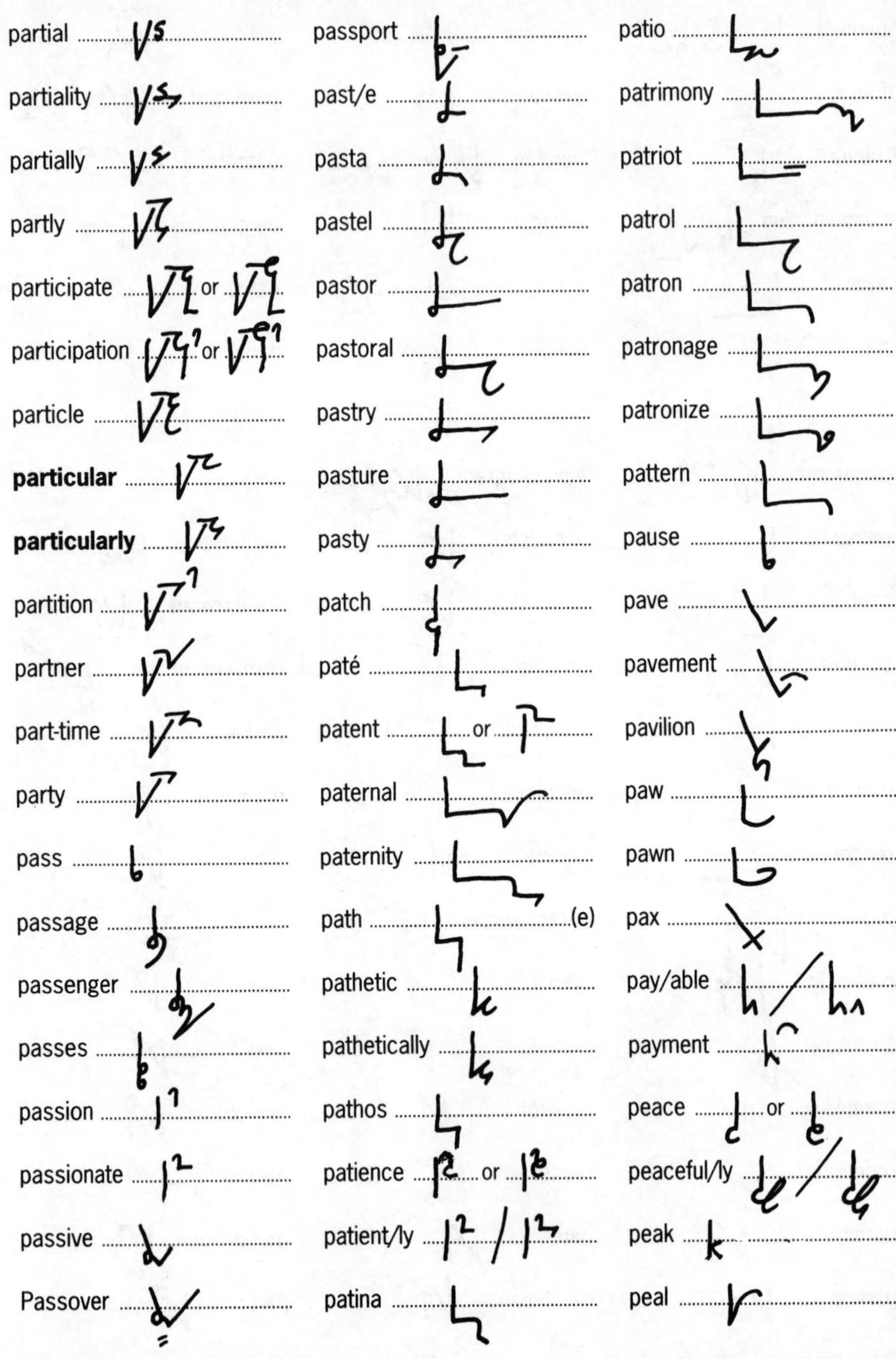

partial
partiality
partially
partly
participate ... or ...
participation ... or ...
particle
particular
particularly
partition
partner
part-time
party
pass
passage
passenger
passes
passion
passionate
passive
Passover

passport
past/e
pasta
pastel
pastor
pastoral
pastry
pasture
pasty
patch
paté
patent ... or ...
paternal
paternity
path ... (e)
pathetic
pathetically
pathos
patience ... or ...
patient/ly ... / ...
patina

patio
patrimony
patriot
patrol
patron
patronage
patronize
pattern
pause
pave
pavement
pavilion
paw
pawn
pax
pay/able ... / ...
payment
peace ... or ...
peaceful/ly ... / ...
peak
peal

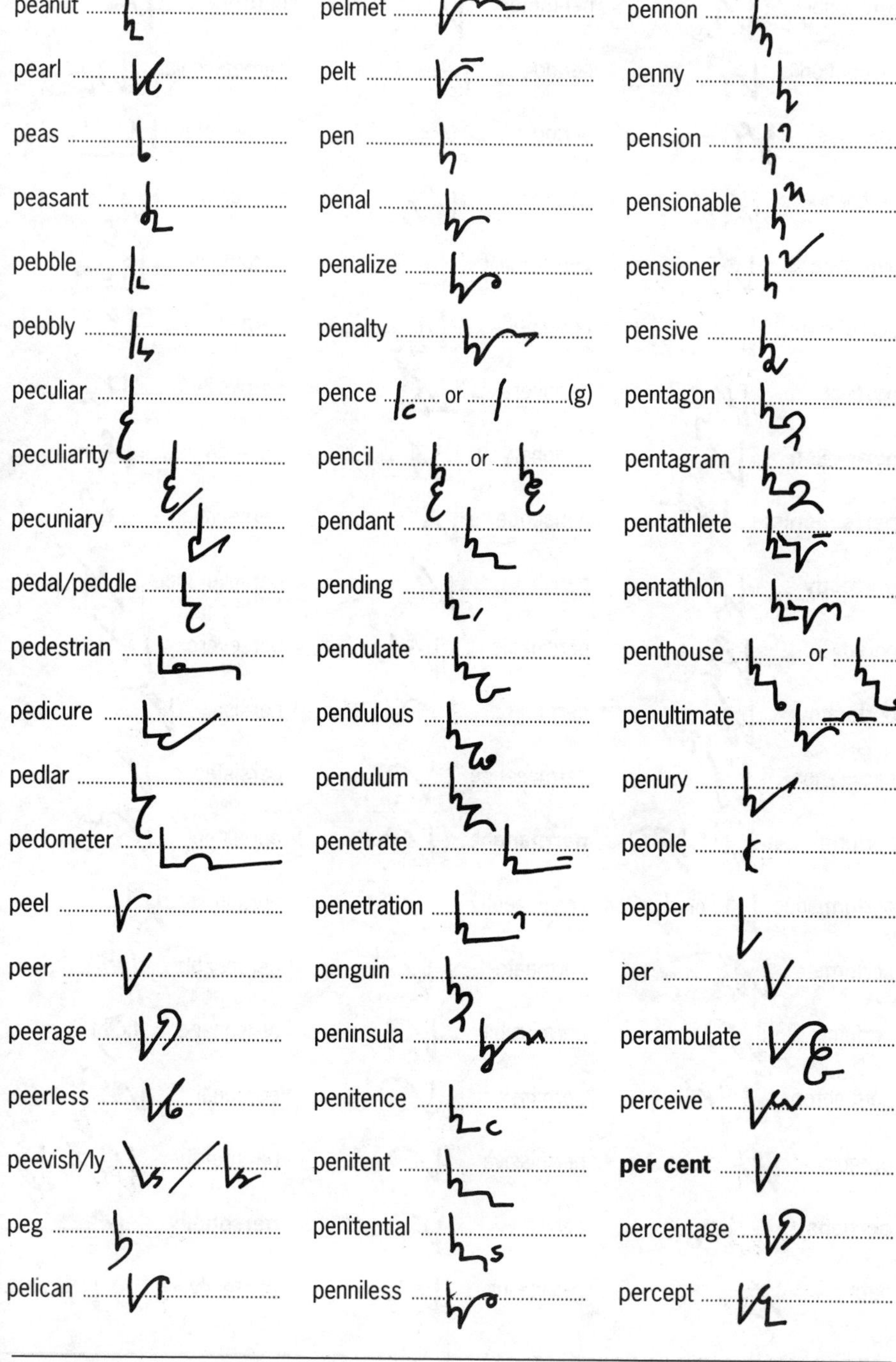

peanut
pearl
peas
peasant
pebble
pebbly
peculiar
peculiarity
pecuniary
pedal/peddle
pedestrian
pedicure
pedlar
pedometer
peel
peer
peerage
peerless
peevish/ly
peg
pelican
pelmet
pelt
pen
penal
penalize
penalty
pence or (g)
pencil or
pendant
pending
pendulate
pendulous
pendulum
penetrate
penetration
penguin
peninsula
penitence
penitent
penitential
penniless
pennon
penny
pension
pensionable
pensioner
pensive
pentagon
pentagram
pentathlete
pentathlon
penthouse or
penultimate
penury
people
pepper
per
perambulate
perceive
per cent
percentage
percept

perceptible

perception

perch

perchance

percolate

percussion

perfect

perfection

perfectionist

perfectly

perfidy

perforate

perforation

perform or

performance or

performer

perfume

perfunctory

pergola

perhaps

peril

perimeter

period

periodic

periodical

periodically

peripatetic

peripheral

periphery

periscope

perish

perishable

perm

permanence

permanent

permanently

permeate

permissible

permission

permissive

permit

pernicious

peroxide

perpendicular

perpetrate

perpetual

perpetuate

perplex

perplexity

persecute

persecution

perseverance

persevere

persist

persistence

persistent

person

personable

personage

personal

personality

personally

personify

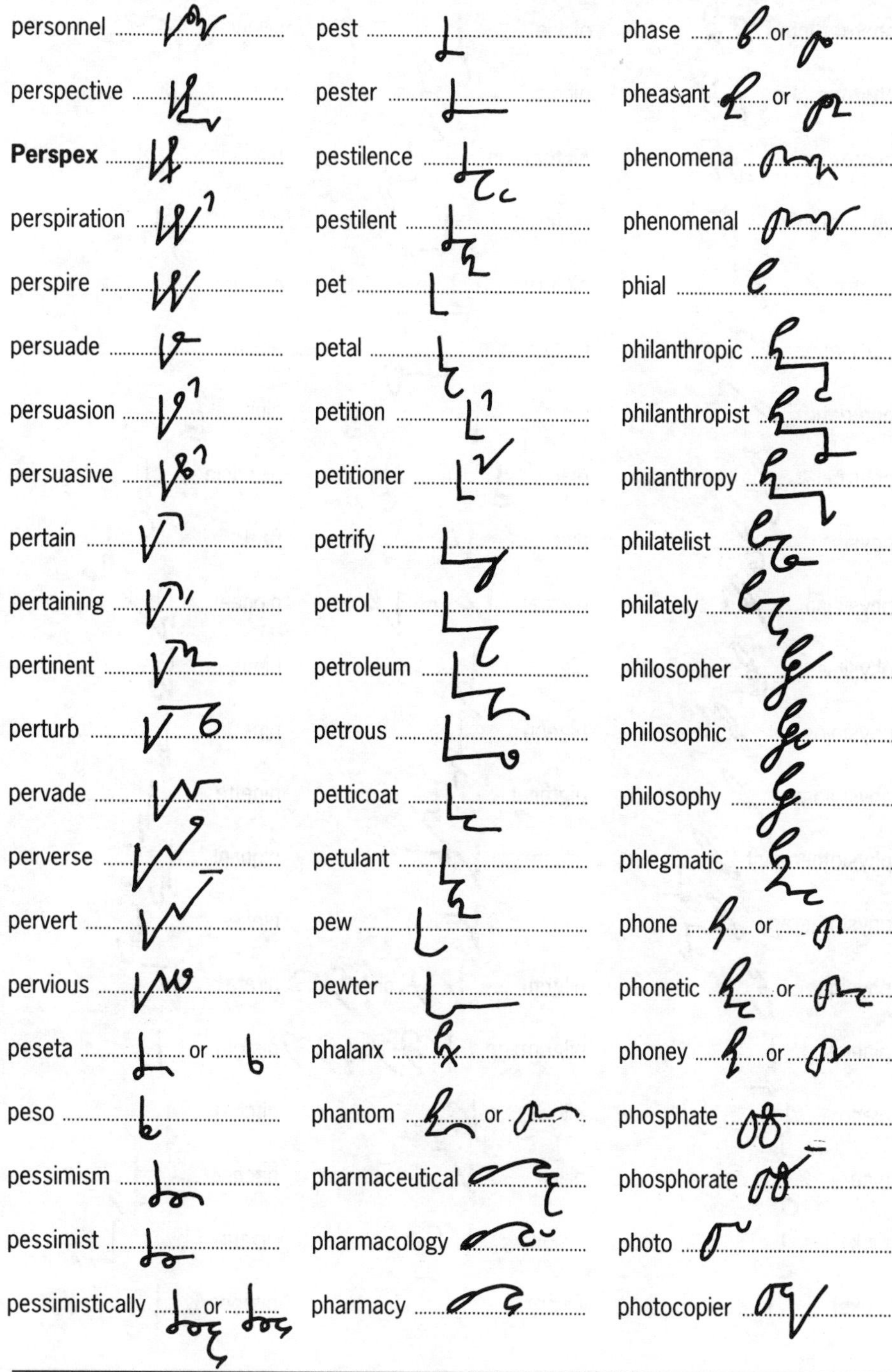
personnel
perspective
Perspex
perspiration
perspire
persuade
persuasion
persuasive
pertain
pertaining
pertinent
perturb
pervade
perverse
pervert
pervious
peseta or
peso
pessimism
pessimist
pessimistically or
pest
pester
pestilence
pestilent
pet
petal
petition
petitioner
petrify
petrol
petroleum
petrous
petticoat
petulant
pew
pewter
phalanx
phantom or
pharmaceutical
pharmacology
pharmacy
phase or
pheasant or
phenomena
phenomenal
phial
philanthropic
philanthropist
philanthropy
philatelist
philately
philosopher
philosophic
philosophy
phlegmatic
phone or
phonetic or
phoney or
phosphate
phosphorate
photo
photocopier

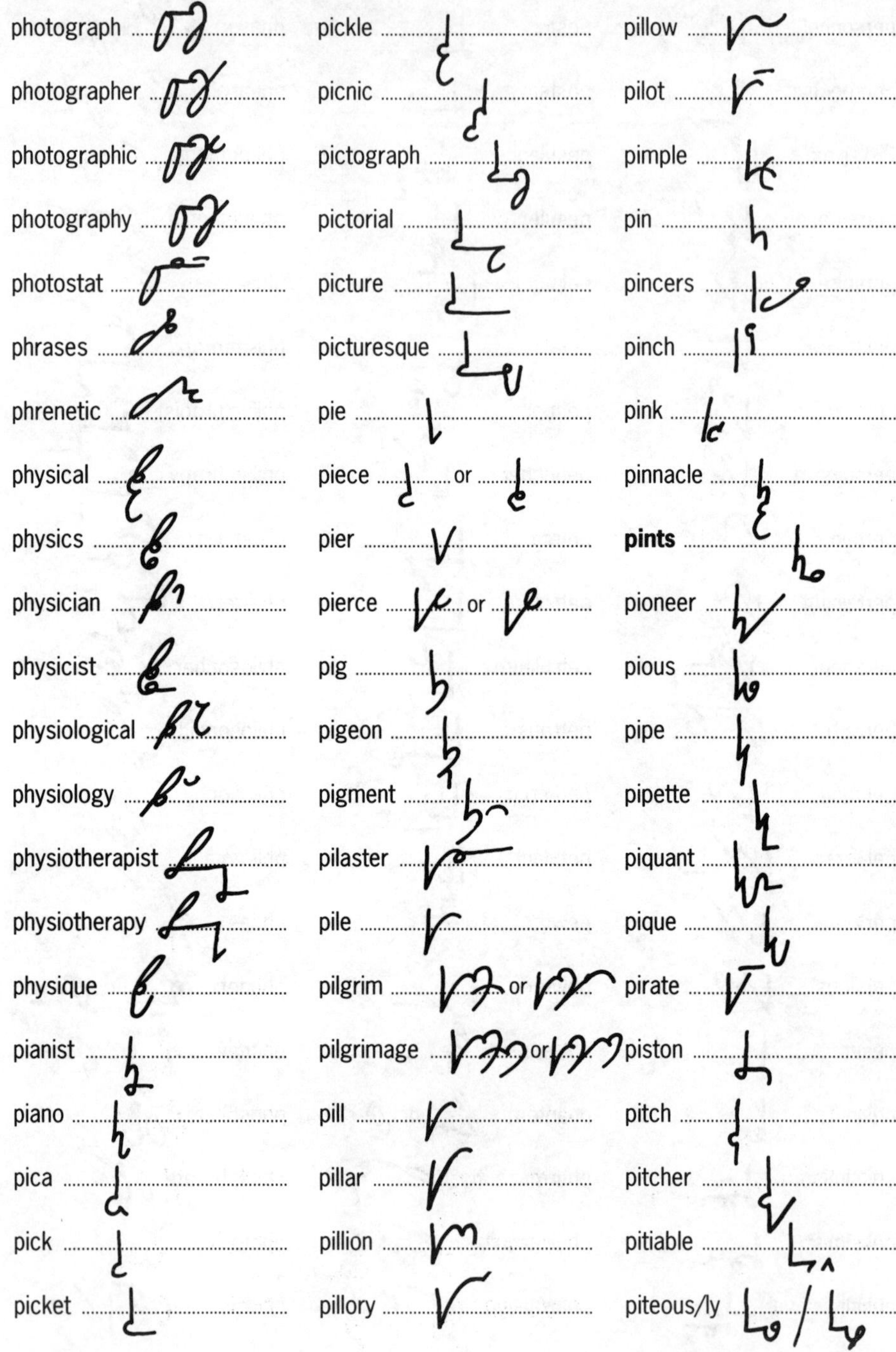

photograph
photographer
photographic
photography
photostat
phrases
phrenetic
physical
physics
physician
physicist
physiological
physiology
physiotherapist
physiotherapy
physique
pianist
piano
pica
pick
picket

pickle
picnic
pictograph
pictorial
picture
picturesque
pie
piece or
pier
pierce or
pig
pigeon
pigment
pilaster
pile
pilgrim or
pilgrimage or
pill
pillar
pillion
pillory

pillow
pilot
pimple
pin
pincers
pinch
pink
pinnacle
pints
pioneer
pious
pipe
pipette
piquant
pique
pirate
piston
pitch
pitcher
pitiable
piteous/ly

pith
pittance
pivot
pixie
pizza ... or ...
placable
placard
placate
place
placebo
placid
plague
plain
plainly
plaintive
plan
plane
planet
planetarium
planetary
plank

plankton
planner
plant
plantation
planter
plaster
plastic
plasticine
plate
plateau
plateful
platform
platinum
platitude
platonic
platoon
plausible
play
player
playground ... or ...
playgroup ... or ...

plaza
plea
plead
pleasant
pleasantly
please
pleasurable
pleasure
plectrum
pledge
plentiful
plenty
pliable
pliant
pliers
plight
plinth
plod
plot
plough
pluck

plucky
plug
plum
plumage
plummet
plump
plunder
plunge or
plunger or
plural or
pluralism or
plurality
plus
plush
plutocracy
plywood or
pneumatic
poach
pocket
podium
poem

poet
poetical
poetry
poignant or
point
pointer
pointless
poisons
poisonous or
polar
polarity
polarize
police
policeman
policy
polish
polite
political
politician
politics
polka

pollen
pollinate
pollute
pollution
polyester
polyglot
polygon
polytechnic or
polyurethane
pompous or
pond
ponder
ponderous
pontificate
pontify
pony
pool
poor
poorly
poorest
pop

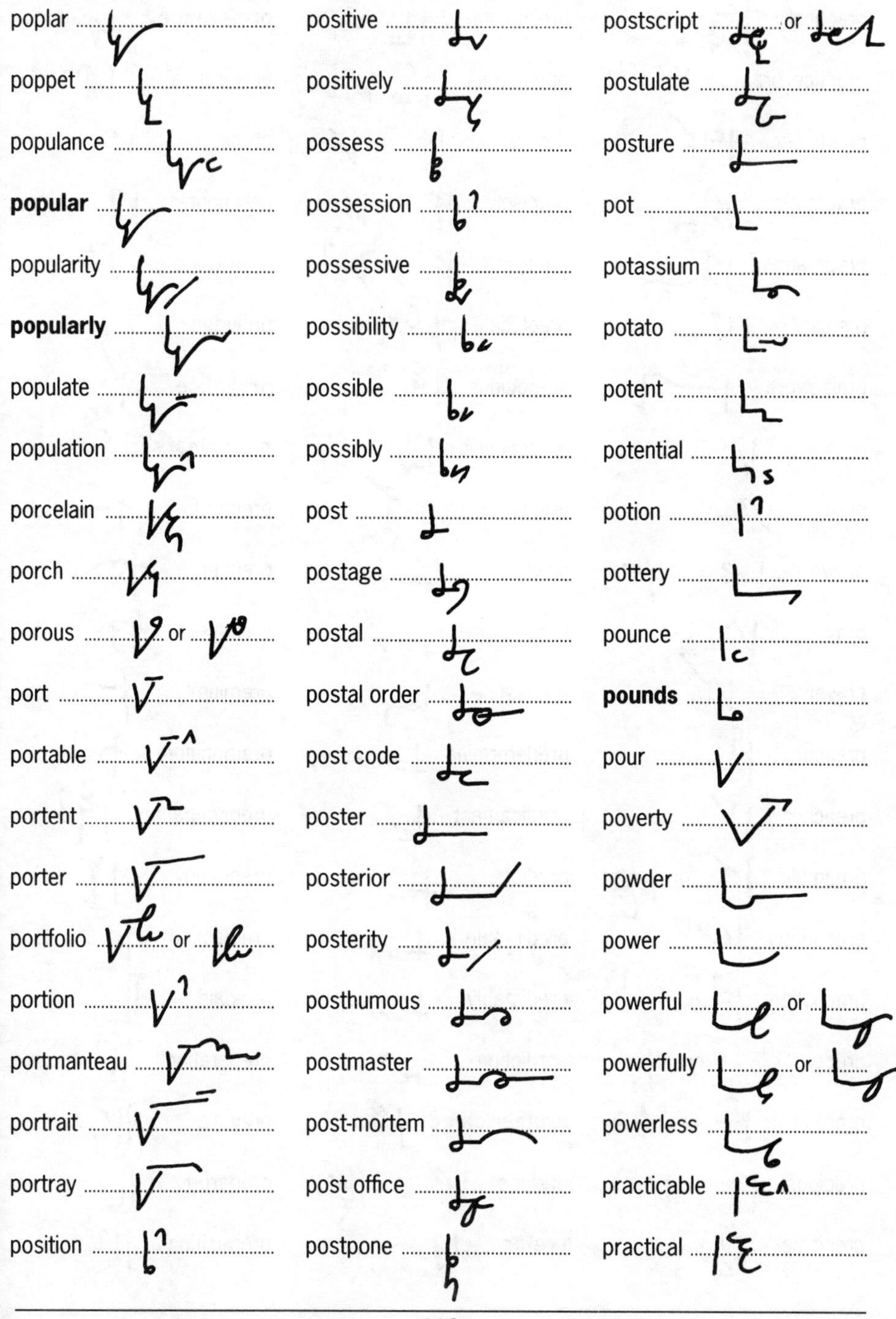

poplar
poppet
populance
popular
popularity
popularly
populate
population
porcelain
porch
porous ... or
port
portable
portent
porter
portfolio ... or
portion
portmanteau
portrait
portray
position

positive
positively
possess
possession
possessive
possibility
possible
possibly
post
postage
postal
postal order
post code
poster
posterior
posterity
posthumous
postmaster
post-mortem
post office
postpone

postscript ... or
postulate
posture
pot
potassium
potato
potent
potential
potion
pottery
pounce
pounds
pour
poverty
powder
power
powerful ... or
powerfully ... or
powerless
practicable
practical

practically

practice/practise ... or ...

practitioner

pragmatic

pragmatism

praise

praiseworthy

prance

prank

prawn ... or ...

pray

prayer

preach

preacher

preamble ... or ...

precarious

precaution ... or ...

precede ... or ...

precinct ... or ...

precious ... or ...

precipice

precipitate

precipitous

precise ... or ...

precisely ... or ...

precision ... or ...

preclude

precocious

preconceive

precursor

predator

predatory

predestine

predetermine

predicament

predict

predictable

predictably

prediction

prefabricated

preface ... or ...

prefer

preference

preferential

prefix

pregnant

prehistoric

prejudge

prejudice

preliminary

premature

premier

premises

premium

premonition

preoccupation

preoccupy

pre-packed

pre-paid

preparation

prepare

prepared

preposition

preposterous or
prerequisite
prerogative
prescribe
prescription
prescriptive
presence
present
presentation
presenter
presently
present-time
preservation
preservative
preserve
preside
president
presidential
press
pressure
Prestel

prestige
presume
presumption
pretence
pretend
pretension
pretext
prettier
prettiest
pretty
prevail
prevalence
prevalent
prevaricate
prevent
prevention
preview
previous
previously
price or
price-list

prick
pride
priest
primary
primate
prime
Prime Minister
primeval
prince
princess
principal/principle
print
printer
prior
priority
prism
prison
prisoner
pristine
privacy
private

privately ....

privilege ....

prize ....

prizes ....

probability ....

probable ....

probably ....

probate ....

probation .... or ....

probationer .... or ....

problem ....

problematical .... or ....

procedure ....

proceed/ings ....

process ....

processes ....

procession .... or ....

processor ....

proclaim ....

procrastinate ....

procure ....

prod ....

prodigal ....

prodigality ....

produce ....

production ....

productive ....

productivity ....

profess ....

profession ....

professional ....

professor ....

proficient ....

profile ....

profit ....

profitable ....

pro forma ....

profuse ....

prognosis ....

prognosticate ....

programme ....

programmer ....

progress ....

progression ....

progressive ....

prohibit ....

prohibition ....

prohibitive ....

project ....

projection ....

projector ....

proliferate ....

prolific ....

prologue ....

prolong .... or ....

promenade ....

prominence ....

prominent ....

prominently ....

promise ....

promontory ....

promote ....

promoter ....

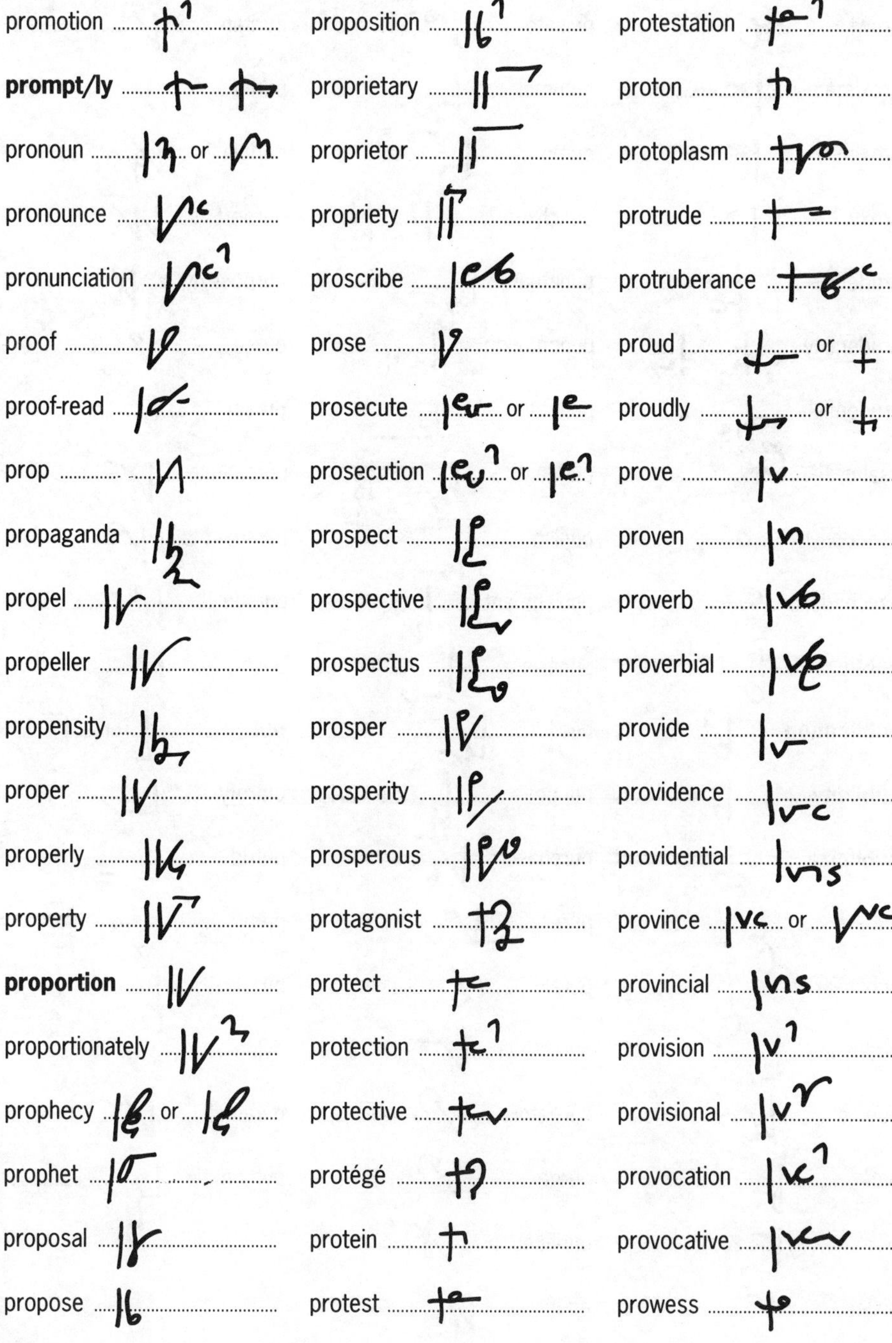

promotion
prompt/ly
pronoun or
pronounce
pronunciation
proof
proof-read
prop
propaganda
propel
propeller
propensity
proper
properly
property
proportion
proportionately
prophecy or
prophet
proposal
propose

proposition
proprietary
proprietor
propriety
proscribe
prose
prosecute or
prosecution or
prospect
prospective
prospectus
prosper
prosperity
prosperous
protagonist
protect
protection
protective
protégé
protein
protest

protestation
proton
protoplasm
protrude
protuberance
proud or
proudly or
prove
proven
proverb
proverbial
provide
providence
providential
province or
provincial
provision
provisional
provocation
provocative
prowess

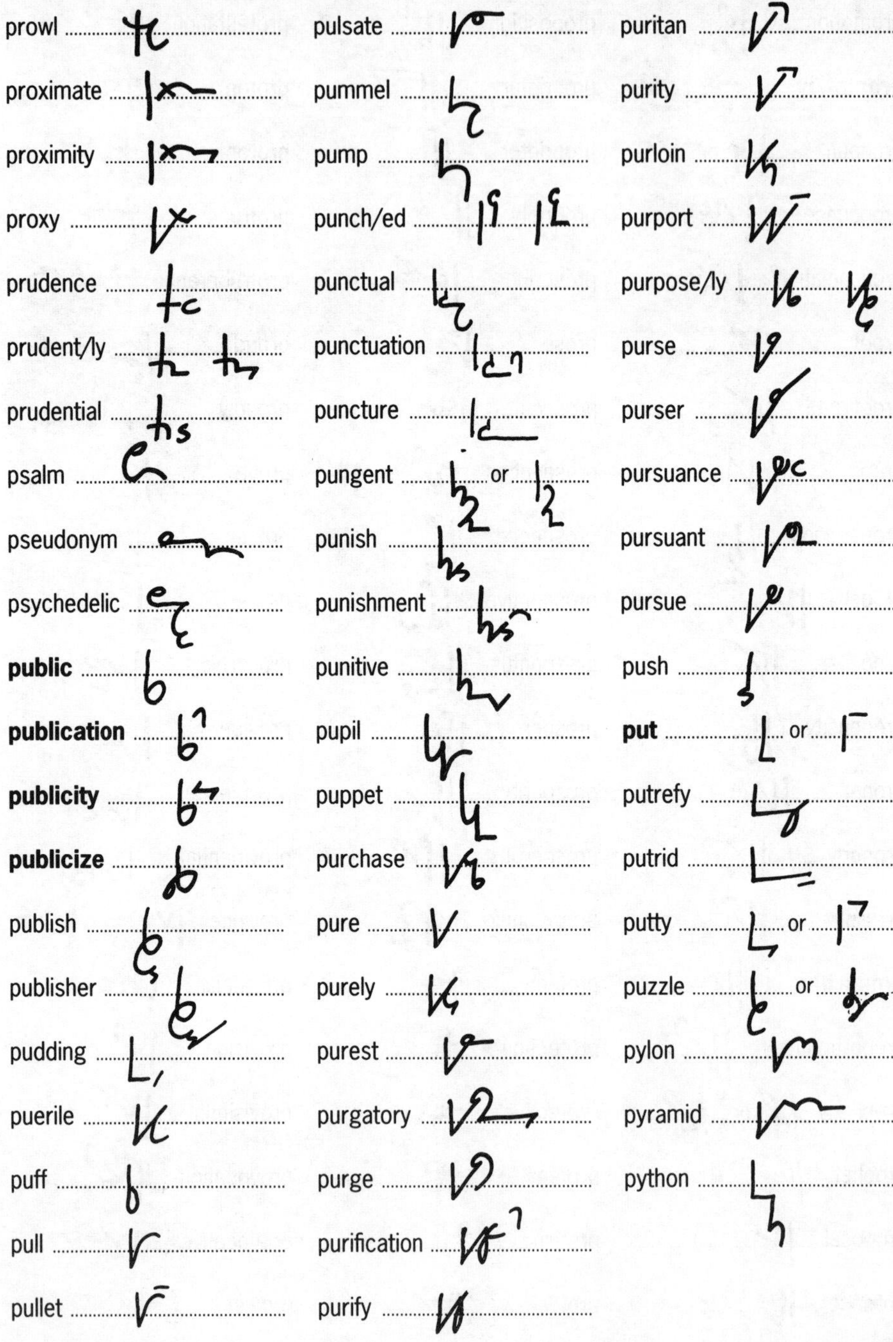

prowl
proximate
proximity
proxy
prudence
prudent/ly
prudential
psalm
pseudonym
psychedelic
public
publication
publicity
publicize
publish
publisher
pudding
puerile
puff
pull
pullet
pulsate
pummel
pump
punch/ed
punctual
punctuation
puncture
pungent or
punish
punishment
punitive
pupil
puppet
purchase
pure
purely
purest
purgatory
purge
purification
purify
puritan
purity
purloin
purport
purpose/ly
purse
purser
pursuance
pursuant
pursue
push
put or
putrefy
putrid
putty or
puzzle or
pylon
pyramid
python

quack
quadrant
quadruped
quaff
quail
quake
qualification
qualified
qualify ... or ...
quality
qualm
quandary
quango
quantative
quantity
quarantine
quarrel
quarry
quart
quarter
quarterly
quartz
quaver
queen ... or ...
queer
quell
quench
query
quest
question
questionable
questionnaire
queue
quibble
quiche
quick ... or ...
quicken
quickly
quid
quiet
quietly ... or ...
quill
quilt
quince
quip
quire
quirk
quit/e
quiver
quiz
quorum
quota
quotation
quote
quotient ... or ...

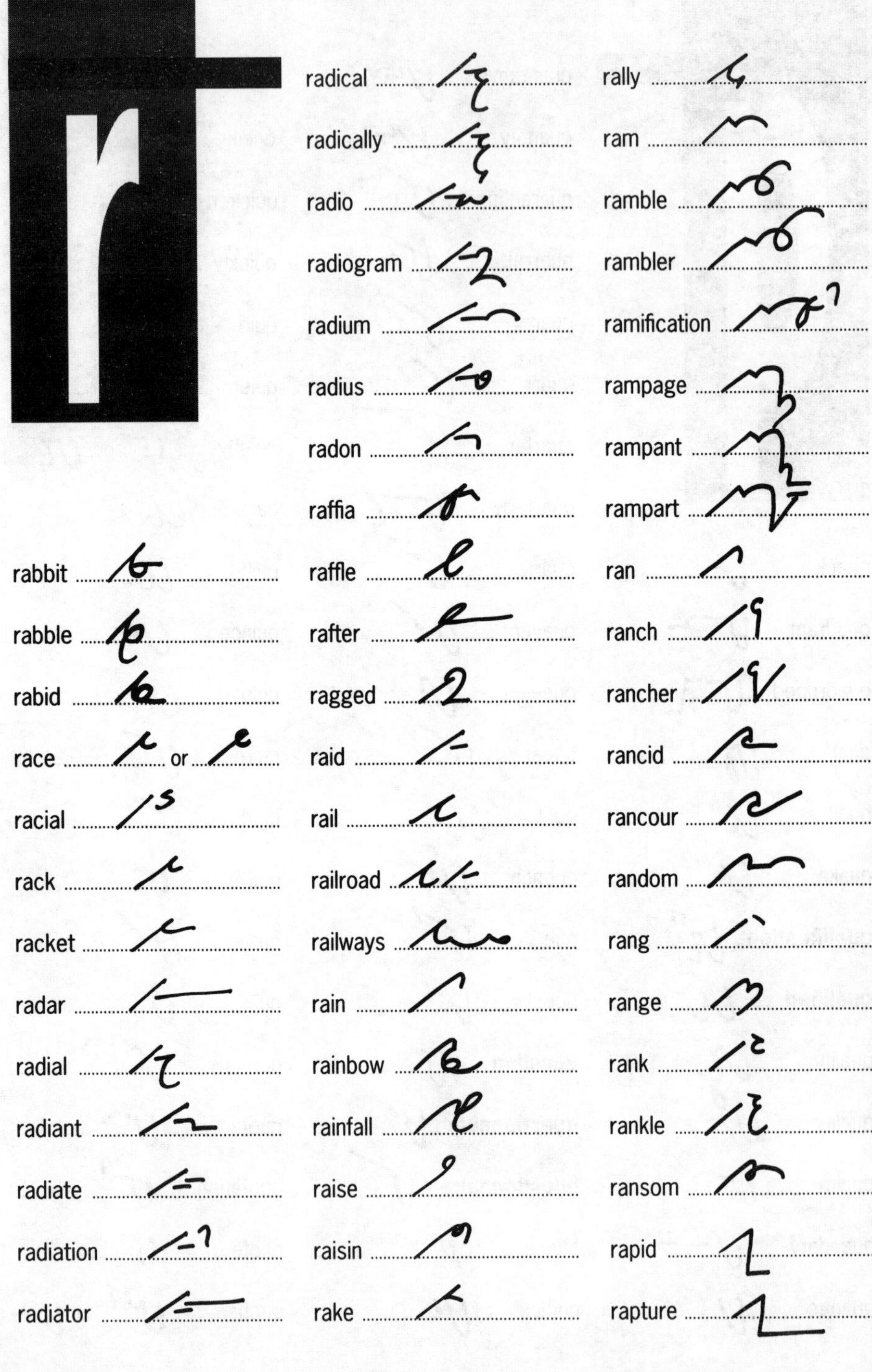

r

rabbit
rabble
rabid
race or
racial
rack
racket
radar
radial
radiant
radiate
radiation
radiator
radical
radically
radio
radiogram
radium
radius
radon
raffia
raffle
rafter
ragged
raid
rail
railroad
railways
rain
rainbow
rainfall
raise
raisin
rake
rally
ram
ramble
rambler
ramification
rampage
rampant
rampart
ran
ranch
rancher
rancid
rancour
random
rang
range
rank
rankle
ransom
rapid
rapture

rare
rarely
rarity
rascal
rash/ly
rasher
rashness
raspberry
rat/e
rateable
rather
ratify
ratio
ration
rational
rationalize
rattle
rave
ravenous
ravioli
raw

ray
raze
razor
reach
react
reaction
read
readable
reader
readily
readiness
ready
real
realism
realistic
reality
realize or
realizing or
really
realm
reap

rear
reason
reasonable/ably
rebel
rebellion
rebellious
rebound
rebuff
rebuilding
rebut
recall
recant
recede
receipt
receive
recent
recently
receptacle
reception
receptionist
receptive

recess
recession
recipe
recipient
reciprocal ... or ...
recital
recite
reckless
reckon ... or ...
reclaim
recline
recluse
recognition ... or ...
recognizance
recognize
recoil
recollect
recommend
recommendation
recompense
reconcile
recondition
reconnaissance
record
recourse
recover
recovery
recreate ... or ...
recriminate ... or ...
recrimination ... or ...
recruit ... or ...
rectangle
rectify
recumbent
recur
recurrence
recurrent
recycled
red
redeem
redeemer
redemption
redeployment
redevelop
redevelopment
rediffusion
reduce
reduction
redundancies
redundancy
reef
reel
refectory
refer ... or ...
referee
reference
referendum
refine
refinement
reflect
reflection
reflex
reform

reformation
reformer
refrain
refresh
refreshment
refrigerate
refuge
refugee
refund
refurbish
refusal
refuse
refute
regain
regal
regalia
regality
regard/less
regatta
regency
regenerate

regent
regime
regimen
regiment
regimental
regimentation
region
regional
register
registrar
registration
registry
regress
regret
regular
regularly
regulate
regulation
regurgitate
rehabilitate
rehearsal

rehearse
reign/rein
reimburse
reinforce ... or ...
reinforcement ... or ...
reinvest ... or ...
reinvestment ... or ...
reject
rejected
rejection
rejoice
rejuvenate
relapse
relate
relations
relationship
relative/ly
relativity
relax
relaxation
relay

release

relegate

relent

relentless

relevant

reliable

reliability

reliably

relief

relieve

religion

religious

relinquish

relish

reluctant

rely

remain

remainder

remake

remand

remark

remarkable

remedies

remedy

remember

remembrance

remind

reminder

reminiscent

remiss

remission

remit

remittance

remnant

remonstrance

remonstrate

remorse

remote

removable

remove

remunerate

renaissance

render

renegade

renew

renewal

renounce

renown

rent

renunciation or

repair

reparation

repartee

repatriate

repay

repeal

repel

repent

repentance

repercussion

repertoire

repetition

repetitive

replace

replacement

replay

replica

replication

reply

report

reporter

repose

repository

repossess

reprehensible

represent

representation

representative

repress

repression

repressive

reprieve

reprimand

reprint ... or

reprisal

reproach

reproachful

reprobate

reproduce

reproduction

reproof

reprove

reptile

republic

republican

repudiate

repugnance

repugnant

repulse

repulsion

repulsive

reputable

reputation

repute

request

requiem ... or

require

requirement

requisite

requisition

rescue

research

rescind

resemblance

resemble

resent

resentful

reservation

reserve

reservoir

reside

residency

resident

residential

residual

residue

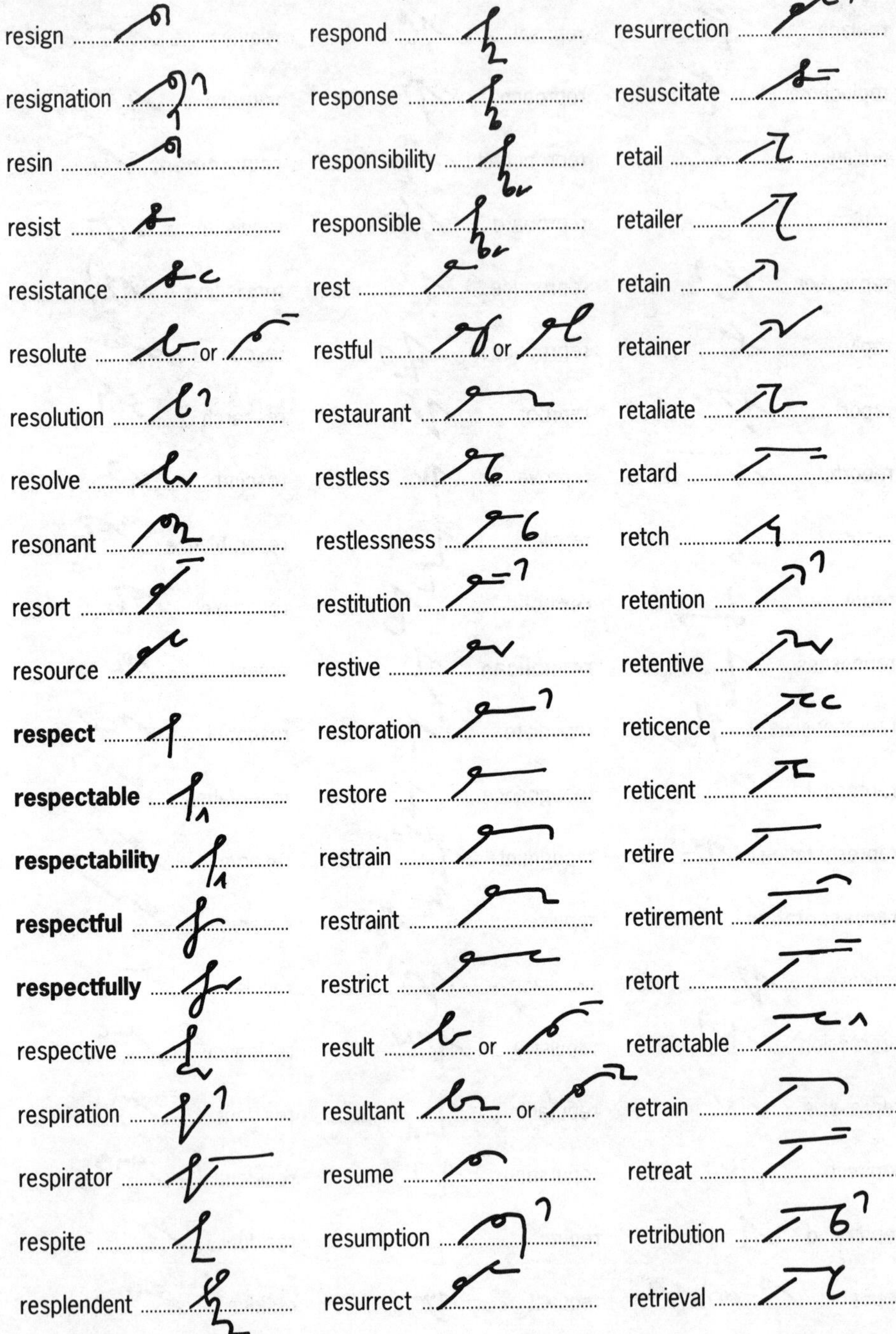

resign
resignation
resin
resist
resistance
resolute ... or ...
resolution
resolve
resonant
resort
resource
respect
respectable
respectability
respectful
respectfully
respective
respiration
respirator
respite
resplendent

respond
response
responsibility
responsible
rest
restful ... or ...
restaurant
restless
restlessness
restitution
restive
restoration
restore
restrain
restraint
restrict
result ... or ...
resultant ... or ...
resume
resumption
resurrect

resurrection
resuscitate
retail
retailer
retain
retainer
retaliate
retard
retch
retention
retentive
reticence
reticent
retire
retirement
retort
retractable
retrain
retreat
retribution
retrieval

retrieve ....
retriever ....
retrograde ....
retrogress ....
retrospect ....
retrospective ....
retrovert ....
return ....
reunion ....
reunite ....
reveal ....
revel ....
revelation ....
revenge ....
revenue ....
reverberate ....
revere ....
reverence ....
reverend ....
reverent ....
reverie ....

reverse ....
reversion ....
revert ....
revertible ....
review ....
revile ....
revise ....
revision ....
revisit ....
revival ....
revive ....
revolt ....
revolution ....
revolutionary ....
revolutionize ....
revolve ....
revolver ....
revue ....
revulsion ....
reward ....
rhapsody ....

rhetoric ....
rhetorical ....
rhubarb ....
rhyme ....
rhythm ....
rib ....
ribald ....
ribbon ....
rice .... or ....
rich ....
riddle ....
rid/e ....
rider ....
ridge ....
ridicule ....
ridiculous ....
rife ....
rifle ....
rift ....
right ....
righteous ....

rightful .... or ....
right-hand ....
rigid ....
rigorous ....
rigour ....
rim ....
rind ....
ring ....
rink ....
riot ....
riposte ....
ripple ....
rise ....
risen ....
risk ....
ritual ....
rival ....
river ....
riverside ....
rivet ....
road ....

roar ....
robin ....
robot ....
robust ....
rock ....
rockery ....
rocket ....
rode ....
rodent ....
rogue ....
roll ....
roller ....
Roman ....
romance ....
romantic ....
romp ....
roof ....
room ....
roomy ....
roost ....
rooster ....

roots ....
rope ....
rose ....
rosette ....
roster ....
rosy ....
rot/e ....
rota ....
rotate ....
rotation ....
rotten ....
rouble ....
rough ....
roughly ....
round .... or ....
routine ....
rove ....
rover ....
row ....
rowdy ....
royal ....

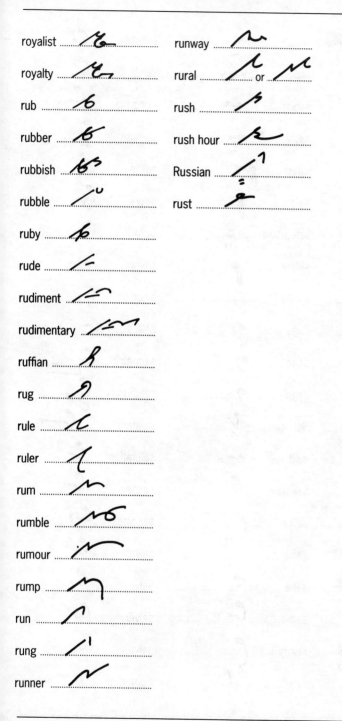

royalist

royalty

rub

rubber

rubbish

rubble

ruby

rude

rudiment

rudimentary

ruffian

rug

rule

ruler

rum

rumble

rumour

rump

run

rung

runner

runway

rural or

rush

rush hour

Russian

rust

S

sabbath

sabbatical

sable

sabotage

saboteur

sabre

sachet

sack

sacrament ... or ...

sacred ... or ...

sacrifice

sacrilege ... or ...

sad

saddle

sadism

sadist

sadly

safari

safe

safeguard

safely

safety

saga

sage

sago

Sahara

said

sail/sale

sailor

saint

sake

salad

salary

sale

saleable

salesman

salesmen

salient

saline

saliva

sallow

salmon

salon

salt

saltpetre

salubrious

salutary

salutation

salute

salvage

salvation

salve

salver

salvo

Samaritan

same
sample
sampler
sanatorium
sanctify ... or ...
sanctimonious
sanction
sanctuary
sand
sandal
sandwich
sang
sane
sanguine
sanitary
sanitation
sanity
sank
sapling
sapphire
sarcasm
sarcastic
sarcophagus
sardine
sardonic
sari
sarong
sash
sat
Satan
satanic
satanism
satchel
satellite
satin
satire
satirical
satirist
satirize
satisfied ... or ...
satisfaction ... or ...
satisfactorily ... or ...
satisfactory ... or ...
satisfy ... or ...
saturate
saturated
saturation
Saturday
Saturn
sauce
saucer
sauna
saunter
sausage
savage
save
savings
saviour
savour
savoury
saw
Saxon
saxophone

say/s ....

scab ....

scabbard ....

scabrous ....

scaffold ....

scaffolding ....

scald ....

scale ....

scallop ....

scalp ....

scalpel ....

scamp ....

scamper ....

scampi ....

scan ....

scandal ....

scandalize ....

scandalous ....

scar/e ....

scarce .... or ....

scarcity ....

scarf ....

scarlet ....

scathing ....

scatter ....

scavenger ....

scene ....

scenery ....

scenic ....

scent ....

sceptic ....

sceptical ....

schedule ....

scheme ....

scholar ....

scholarship ....

scholastic ....

school ....

schoolboy ....

schooner ....

science ....

scientific ....

scientifically ....

scientist ....

scissors ....

scoff ....

scold ....

scone ....

scoop ....

scope ....

scorch ....

score ....

scorpion ....

Scots ....

Scottish ....

scoundrel ....

scour ....

scourge ....

scout ....

scowl ....

scrabble .... or ....

scramble ....

scrap ....

scratch ....
scream ....
screech ....
screen .... or ....
screw .... or ....
scribble ....
scribe ....
scrimp ....
script ....
scripture ....
scroll .... or ....
scrounge .... or ....
scrounger .... or ....
scrub ....
scruff .... or ....
scruple ....
scrutineer ....
scrutinize ....
scuff ....
scuffle ....
scullery ....
sculptor ....
sculpture ....
scupper ....
scurry ....
scuttle ....
scythe ....
sea ....
seaside ....
seal ....
seam ....
seamstress ....
seance ....
sear ....
search ....
season ....
seasonal ....
seat ....
seatbelt ....
seaward ....
seclude ....
seclusion ....
second ....(g)
secondary ....
secondly ....
second-class ....
second-hand ....
secrecy ....
secret ....
secretarial ....
secretary ....
secretly ....
section ....
sector ....
secular ....
secure ....
securities ....
security ....
sedate ....
sedative ....
sedentary ....
sediment ....
seduce .... or ....

seduction

see

seeing

seed

seek

seem

seemingly

seen

seethe

segment

segregate

segregation

seize

select

selection

selective

self (b)

self-confidence

self-confident

self-contained

self-control

self-defence

self-denial

self-employed

self-evident

selfish

selfishly

selfless

self-possessed

self-propelled

self-reliant

self-satisfied

self-service

self-supporting

self-willed

sell

seller

semantics

semblance

semi-automatic

semicircle

semicircular

semicolon

semi-conscious

semi-darkness

semi-detached

seminar

semi-precious

semi-tropical

senate

senator

send

senile

senility

senior

seniority

sensation

sensationalism

sense

senseless

sensibility

sensible

sensibly

sensitive
sensitively
sensitivity
sensual
sensuous
sent
sentence
sentiment
sentimental
sentimentality
sentry
separate
separately
separation
September
septic
sequel
sequence
sequential
serene
serenity

serf
sergeant
serial
serialize
series
serious
seriously
seriousness
sermon
serpent
serpentine
serrate
servant
serve
service
serviceable
serviette
servile
session
set
settle

settlement
seven
seventh
sever
several
severe
severity
sew
sewage
sewer
sex
sexual
sexuality
shabby
shack
shackle
shade
shadow
shady
shaft
shaggy

shake ....

shaken ....

shaker ....

shall ....

shallow ....

sham ....

shambles ....

shame ....

shameful ....

shameless ....

shampoo ....

shank ....

shanty ....

shape ....

shapely ....

share ....

shareholder ....

shark ....

sharp ....

sharpen ....

sharpened ....

sharply ....

sharpness ....

shatter ....

shave ....

shawl ....

she ....

sheaf ....

shear ....

sheath ....

sheaves ....

shed ....

sheen ....

sheep ....

sheepish ....

sheet ....

shelf .... or ....

shell ....

shellfish ....

shelves ....

shepherd ....

sherbet ....

sheriff .... or ....

sherry ....

Shetland ....

shield ....

shift ....

shimmer ....

shin/e ....

shingle ....

ship ....

shipment ....

shire ....

shirk ....

shirt ....

shiver ....

shoal ....

shock ....

shocked ....

shoddy ....

shoe ....

shook ....

shoot ....

shop

shopkeeper ... or ...

shoplifting

shopper

shore

shortage

shorten

shorter

shortest

shorthand

shorthand-typist

shortly

shot

should

shoulders

shout

shove

shovel

show

shower

shown

shrank

shred

shredder

shrew

shrewd

shriek

shrill

shrimp

shrine

shrink

shrinkage

shrivel

shroud

shrub

shrug/ged

shudder

shuffle

shun

shunt

shut

shutter

shuttle

shy

sick

sicken

sickness

side

sideboard

sideways

siege

sieve

sift

sigh

sight

sign

signal

signatory

signature

significance ... or ...

significant/ly

signify

signpost

silence ....

silencer ....

silent ....

silently .... or ....

silicon ....

silk ....

silo ....

silver ....

similar .... or ....

similarity ....

similarly .... or ....

simmer ....

simple ....

simpleton ....

simplicity ....

simplify ....

simply ....

simulate .... or ....

simulation .... or ....

simultaneous .... or ....

sin/e ....

since ....

sincere ....

sincerely .... or ....(g)

sinecure ....

sing ....

singer ....

single ....

singly ....

singular ....

sinister ....

sink ....

sinuate .... or ....

sinuous ....

sip ....

siphon ....

sir ....

sister ....

sit/e ....

sitter ....

situate .... or ....

situated .... or ....

situation ....

six ....

sixteen ....

sixth ....

sixty ....

sizeable ....

size ....

sizzle ....

skate ....

skeleton ....

sketch ....

skewer ....

ski ....

skid ....

skilful ....

skill ....

skim ....

skimp ....

skin ....

skip ....

skipper ....

skirmish
skirt
skittle
skunk
sky
slab
slack
slag
slam
slander
slang
slant
slap
slapdash
slash
slat/e
slaughter
slave
slavery
slavish
sledge

sleek
sleep
sleeper
sleet
sleeve
slender
slice or
slide
slight
slightest
slightly
slim/e
slimmer
sling
slip
slipper
slippery
slipshod
slit
slither
sliver

slog
slogan
slop/e
slot
sloth
sloven
slovenly
slow
slower
slowest
slowly or
slug
sluggard
sluggish
sluice or
slum
slumber or
slump
slur
slurry
slush

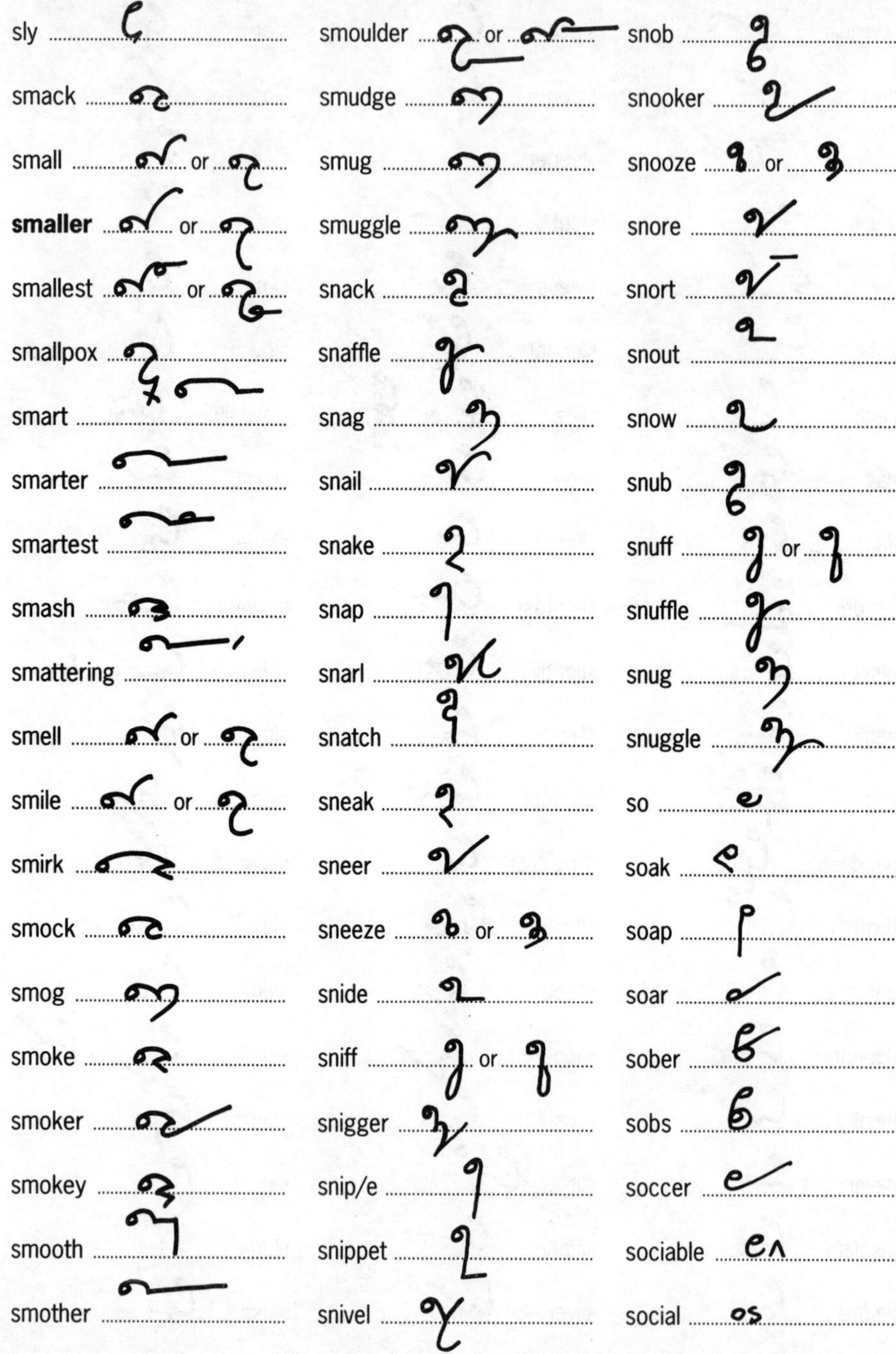

sly
smack
small ... or ...
smaller ... or ...
smallest ... or ...
smallpox
smart
smarter
smartest
smash
smattering
smell ... or ...
smile ... or ...
smirk
smock
smog
smoke
smoker
smokey
smooth
smother
smoulder ... or ...
smudge
smug
smuggle
snack
snaffle
snag
snail
snake
snap
snarl
snatch
sneak
sneer
sneeze ... or ...
snide
sniff ... or ...
snigger
snip/e
snippet
snivel
snob
snooker
snooze ... or ...
snore
snort
snout
snow
snub
snuff ... or ...
snuffle
snug
snuggle
so
soak
soap
soar
sober
sobs
soccer
sociable
social

socialism

socialist

socialize

society

socio-economic

sociological

sociologist

sociology

sock

socket

soda

sodium

sofa

soft

softens

softness

software

soggy

soil

solace ... or ...

solar

solarium

sold

solder

soldier

solemn

solemnity

solicit

solicitor

solid

solidarity

solitary

solo

soluble

solution

solve

solvency

solvent

some

someone ... or ...

somehow

something

sometimes ... or ...

somewhere

son

sonata

song

sonic

sonnet

soon

soot

soothe

sophisticate

sophisticated

sophistication

soprano ... or ...

sordid

sorrow

sorrowful ... or ...

sorry

sort

sought ... or ...

soul

soulful .... or ....
sound .... or ....
soup ....
sour ....
source ....
south/southern ....
souvenir ....
sovereign ....
soviet ....
sow ....
soya ....
space .... or ....
spacious .... or ....
spade ....
spaghetti ....
span ....
spaniel ....
Spanish ....
spank ....
spanner ....
spar/e ....
spark ....
sparkle ....
sparrow ....
sparse ....
spatial ....
spatula ....
spawn ....
speak ....
speaker ....
special ....
specialism ....
specialist ....
speciality ....
specialize ....
specially ....
species .... or ....
specific ....
specifically ....
specification ....
specify ....
specimen ....
speck ....
speckle ....
spectacle ....
spectator ....
spectrum ....
speculation ....
speech ....
speechless ....
speed ....
speedily ....
speedometer ....
spell ....
spend ....
spent ....
sphere ....
spider ....
spike ....
spill ....
spin/e ....
spinach ....
spindle ....

spineless
spinnaker
spinster
spiral
spire
spirit
spiritual
spiritualism
spiritualist
spit/e
spiteful ... or ...
spitefulness
splash
splatter
splendid
splendour
splice ... or ...
splinter
split
spoil
spoke

spoken
spokesman
sponge ... or ...
sponsor
spontaneous
spoof
spool
spoon
spoor
sporadic
sport
sportsman
sportswoman
spot
spotless
spout
sprain
sprawl
spray
spread
spree

spring
sprinkle
sprint ... or ...
sprocket
sprout
spruce ... or ...
sprung
spur
spurious
spurn
spurt
spy
squabble
squad
squadron
squalid
squall
squander
square
squarely
squash

squat
squatter
squawk
squeak
squeal
squeamish
squeeze
squib
squid
squint
squire
squirm
squirrel
squirt
stab
stable
stability
stabilizer
stack
stadium
staff

stag/e
stagger
stagnate
stain
stair
stake
stalactite
stalagmite
stale
stalemate
stalk
stall
stallion
stalwart
stamen
stamina
stammer
stamp
stampede
stance
stand

standard
standardize
stanza
staple
stapler
star/e
starboard
stark
starling
start
startle
starve
state
statement
statesman
statesmen
station
stationary/ery
statistical
statistician
statistics

statuesque ....

status ....

statute ....

statutory ....

staunch ....

stave ....

stay ....

stead ....

steady ....

steal/steel ....

steam ....

steep ....

steeple ....

steer ....

steerage ....

stem ....

stench ....

stencil .... or ....

stenographer ....

stenography ....

step ....

stereo ....

stereotype ....

sterile ....

sterling ....

stern ....

stew ....

steward ....

stick ....

sticker ....

stickler ....

stiff ....

stiffen ....

stiffer ....

stifle ....

stigma ....

stigmatize ....

still/stile ....

stilt ....

stimulant ....

stimulate ....

stimulation ....

stimulus ....

sting ....

stink ....

stipulate ....

stitch ....

stoat ....

stock ....

stockbroker ....

stockist ....

stock-market ....

stomach ....

stone ....

stony ....

stood ....

stop ....

stoppage ....

storage ....

store ....

storey/story ....

stormy ....

stove ....

stow	stream	strong
straddle	street	stronger
straight	strength	strongest
straightforward	strengthen	strongly
strain	strenuous	structure
strand	stress	struggle
strange ... or ...	stretch	strung
strangely	stretcher	strut
stranger	strict	stub
strangest	strictest	stubble
strangle	stride	stubborn
strangulate	strident	student
strap	strike	studied
stratagem	string	studio
strategic	stringent	study
strategically	strip/e	stuff
strategy	striped	stumble ... or ...
stratum	strive	stump
strawberry	strode	stunt
stray	stroke	stupefy
streak	stroll	stupendous

stupid
sturdy
stutter
sty
style
stylist
stylistic
stylize ... or ...
stylus
subdivide
subdue
sub-editor
subject
subjection
subjective
sublime
submarine
submerge
submission
submit
subordinate

subscribe ... or ...
subscriber
subscription ... or ...
subsequent/ly
subservience
subservient
subside
subsidence
subsidiary
subsidize
subsidy
subsist
subsistence
subsistent
subsoil
substance
substantial
substantiate
substitute
subsume
subterfuge

subtle
subtlety
subtract
suburb
suburban
subvert
subzero
succeed ... or ...
success
successful
succession
successive
successor
succinct ... or ...
succour
succulent
succumb
such
suck
suckle
suction

sudden
suddenly
sue/d
suede
suet
suffer
suffered
sufferance
suffice
sufficiency
sufficient
sufficiently
suffix
suffocate
sugar
suggest
suggestion
suggestive
suicide
suit/e
suitable

suitor ... or ...
sulk
sullen
sulphur
sultan
sultry
sum
summarize
summary
summer
summit
sumptuous
sun
Sunday
sunset
sundry
sung
sunlight
sunshine
super ... (b)
superannuation

superb
superficial
superfluous
superhuman
superintendent ... or ...
superior
superiority ... or ...
supermarket
supernatural
supersede
supersonic
superstition
superstitious
supertax
supervise
supervision
supervisor
supper
supple
supplement
supplementary

supplier
supplies
supply
support
supporter
supportive
suppose/d
supposition
supremacy
sure
surely
surf
surface or
surge
surgeon
surgery
surgical
surmise
surmount
surname
surpass

surplus
surprise
surrender
surreptitous
surrogate
surround
surtax
surveillance
survey
surveyor
survival
survive
susceptible
suspect
suspense
suspension
suspicion
suspicious
sustain
sustenance
swag

swagger
swallow
swam
swan
swarm
sway
swear
sweat
sweep
sweet
sweetheart
swell
swerve
swift
swim
swimmer
swimwear
swindle
swing
switch
switch-over or

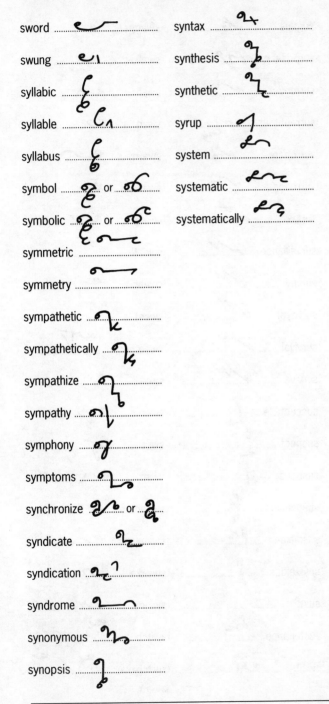

sword ....

swung ....

syllabic ....

syllable ....

syllabus ....

symbol .... or ....

symbolic .... or ....

symmetric ....

symmetry ....

sympathetic ....

sympathetically ....

sympathize ....

sympathy ....

symphony ....

symptoms ....

synchronize .... or ....

syndicate ....

syndication ....

syndrome ....

synonymous ....

synopsis ....

syntax ....

synthesis ....

synthetic ....

syrup ....

system ....

systematic ....

systematically ....

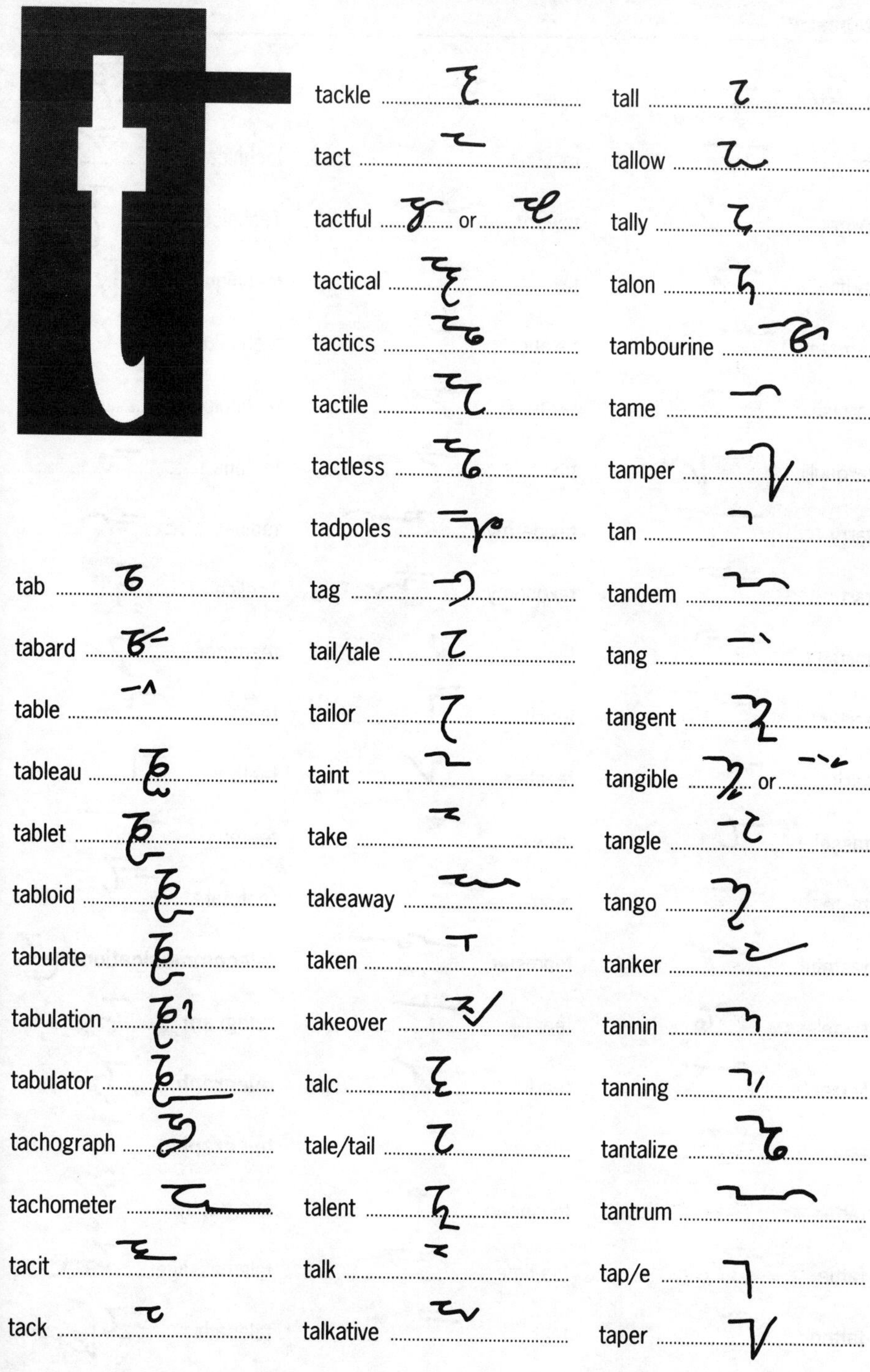

tab

tabard

table

tableau

tablet

tabloid

tabulate

tabulation

tabulator

tachograph

tachometer

tacit

tack

tackle

tact

tactful or

tactical

tactics

tactile

tactless

tadpoles

tag

tail/tale

tailor

taint

take

takeaway

taken

takeover

talc

tale/tail

talent

talk

talkative

tall

tallow

tally

talon

tambourine

tame

tamper

tan

tandem

tang

tangent

tangible or

tangle

tango

tanker

tannin

tanning

tantalize

tantrum

tap/e

taper

tapestry ....
tar ....
target ....
tariff ....
tarmac ....
tarnish ....
tarpaulin ....
tarry ....
tart ....
tartan ....
tartar ....
task ....
tassel ....
taste ....
tasteful ....
tasteless ....
taster ....
tasty ....
tatter ....
tattle ....
tattoo ....

taunt ....
taut ....
tawdry ....
tax ....
taxation ....
tax-free ....
taxi ....
taxidermy ....
taxonomy ....
tea ....
teach ....
teacher ....
teak ....
team ....
teamster ....
tear ....
tearful ....
tease ....
teaspoon ....
tea-time ....
teat ....

technical ....
technicality ....
Technicolour ....
technique ....
technological .... or ....
technology .... or ....
tedious ....
tedium ....
Teeline ....
teenager ....
teens ....
teeth ....
teeter ....
teetotal ....
telecommunications ....
telegram ....
telegraph ....
telegraphic ....
telegraphy ....
telemessage ....
telepathic ....

telepathy

telephone

telephonist

teleprinter

telescope

telescopic

Teletext

television or

telex

tell

teller

telltale

temerity

temper

temperament

temperamental

temperance

temperate

temperature

tempest

tempestuous

template

temple

temporary or

tempt or

temptation or

ten

tenable

tenacious

tenant

tend

tendency

tender

tendon

tendril

tenement

tenet

tennis

tenon

tenor

tense

tension

tent

tentacle

tentative

tenuous

tenure

tepid

term

terminable

terminal

terminate

termination

terminator

terminology

terminus

termite

terrace

terrain

terrestrial

terrible

terribly

terrier

terrific	thatch	thereby
territorial	thaw	**therefore**
territory	**the**	therm
terror	theatre	thermal
terrorist	theatrical	thermometer
terrorize	theft	Thermos
terse	their/there (g)	**these**
tertiary	them	thesis
Terylene	theme	**they**
test	themselves	thick
testament	then	thicken
tether	thence	thicker
text or	theodolite	thickness
textile or	theology	thief
texture or	theoretical	thieves
than	theory	thigh
thank (g)	therapeutic	thimble or
thankful	therapist	thin
thankfulness	therapy (e)	thing (g)
thanklessness	there/their (g)	think (g)
that	**thereafter**	thinker

third
thirst
thirteen
thirty
this
thistle
thong
thorough
thoroughly or
those
though
thought
thoughtful
thoughtfulness
thoughtless
thoughtlessness
thousand (g)
thrash
thread
threat
threaten

three or
threesome
threshold or
threw
thrift or
thrill
thrive
throat
throb
throne
throng
throttle
through or
throughout
throw
thrown
thrush
thrust
thud
thug
thumb

thumbnail
thump
thunder
Thursday
thus
thwart
tick
ticket
tickle
tickler
ticklish
tidal
tide
tidy
tie
tiff
tiger
tight
tightly or
tile
till

tiller/tiler ....

tilt ....

timber .... or ....

time .... or ....

timetable ....

timeless ....

timid ....

timorous ....

tin ....

tincture .... or ....

tinder ....

tinge ....

tingle ....

tinker ....

tinkle ....

tinny ....

tinsel ....

tint ....

tiny ....

tip ....

tipple ....

tipsy ....

tirade ....

tire/tyre ....

tired ....

tireless ....

tiresome ....

tissue ....

titillate ....

title ....

to ....

toad ....

toast ....

tobacco ....

today ....

toddle ....

toe ....

tog ....

toga ....

together ....

toggle ....

toil ....

toilet ....

token ....

tolerable ....

tolerant ....

tolerate ....

toleration ....

told ....

tomb ....

tomato ....

tombola ....

tomorrow ....

ton/tonne ....

tongue .... or ....

tonic ....

tonight ....

tonnage ....

too ....

took ....

tool ....

toolkit .... or ....

tooth ....

toothache ....

top ....

topical ....

topaz ....

topic ....

topple ....

torch ....

torment ....

tormentor ....

tornado ....

torpedo ....

torque ....

torrential ....

torsion ....

torso ....

tort ....

tortoise ....

torture ....

Tory ....

toss ....

total/ly ....

totalitarian ....

totem ....

touch ....

tough ....

tour .... or ....

tourist .... or ....

tournament ....

tow ....

towards ....

tower .... or ....

town ....

township ....

toxic ....

toxin ....

toy ....

trace ....

tracer ....

track ....

tract ....

tractable ....

traction ....

tractor ....

trade ....

trader ....

tradesman ....

tradesmen ....

tradition ....

traditional ....

traditionally ....

traffic ....

tragedy ....

tragic ....

trail ....

trailer ....

train ....

trainee ....

trainer ....

trait ....

traitor ....

tram ....

tramp ....

trample ....

trampoline	translate	travel
trance	translation	traveller
tranquil	translator	travelling
tranquility	translucent	traverse
tranquillizer	transmission	travesty
transaction	transmit	trawl
transatlantic	transmitter	trawler
transcribe	transpire	tray
transcription	transplant	treacherous
transfer	transport	tread
transference	transporter	treadle
transferable	transportation	treason
transfix	transpose	treasure
transform	transposition	treasurer
transformation	trans-ship	treasury
transformer	trans-shipment	treat
transgress	transverse	treatise
transistor	trap	treatment
transit	trapper	treaty
transition	trash	treble
transitory	travail	trebly

tree ....

trek ....

trellis ....

tremble ....

tremendous ....

tremor ....

tremulous ....

trench ....

trend ....

trepidation ....

trestle ....

triad ....

trial ....

triangle ....

triangular ....

tribal ....

tribe ....

tribunal ....

tribune .... or ....

tributary ....

tribute ....

trick ....

trickle ....

tricycle ....

tried ....

trifle .... or ....

trigger ....

trilby ....

trill ....

trilogy ....

trim ....

trinity ....

trinket ....

trip/e ....

triple ....

triplet ....

triplex ....

triplicate ....

tripod ....

triumph ....

triumphant ....

trivet ....

trivial ....

trolley ....

trombone ....

troop ....

trophy ....

tropic ....

tropical ....

trot ....

trotter ....

trouble ....

troubled ....

trough ....

trousers ....

trowel ....

truant ....

truck ....

truculent ....

true ....

truffle .... or ....

truly ....

trumpet ....

truncheon

trundle

trunk

trust

trustee

trustworthy

truth

truthful

truthfully

try

trying

tubular

tuck

Tuesday

tuft

tug

tuition

tulip

tumble

tumbler

tumour

tuna

tundra

tune

tuneful

tuneless ... or ...

tungsten ... or ...

tunic

tunnel

turban

turbot

turbulent

turf

turkey

Turkish

turmoil

turn

turnover

turnip

turpentine

turquoise

turret

turtle

tusk

tussle

tussock

tutor

tutorial

TV

twaddle

twang

tweed

tweak

tweezers

twelfth ... or 12]

twelve ... or 12

twenty ... or 20

twice ... or ...

twiddle

twig

twilight

twill

twin

twinge .... or ....

twinkle ....

twirl ....

twist ....

twister ....

twitch ....

two .... or ....

type ....

typewriter ....

typhoon ....

typical ....

typify ....

typist ....

tyrannical ....

tyranny ....

tyrant ....

ubiquitous

ubiquity

udder

ugly

ulcer

ulcerate

ullage

ulterior

Ulster

ultimate

ultimatum

ultra (b)

ultramodern

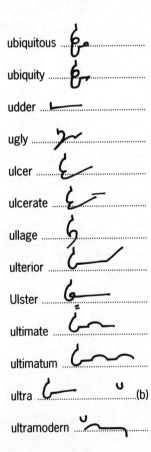

ultraviolet

umbel or

umber or

umbles or

umbrage or

umbrella or

umpire

umpteen

unable

unaccompanied

unalterable

unanimous

unbiased

unceasing

unceasingly

uncertain

uncertainly

uncertainty

uncle

uncomfortable

uncommon

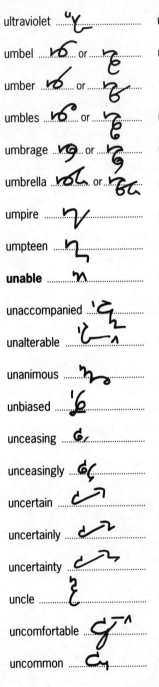

uncommunicative

uncomplicated

uncomplimentary

unconcerned

unconscious

unconstitutional

uncontaminated

uncontrollable

uncouth

uncover

uncross

uncurl

under (b)

undercurrent

undergo

undergone

undergraduate

underground

underhand

under-insured

underline

underlying
undermine
underpass
underprivileged
understand
understood
understudy
undertake
undertaken
undertaker
undertook
underwrite
underwriter
undo
undoubted/ly
undulate
unearth
uneconomic
uneconomical
unemployed
unemployment

unethical
unexpected
unfasten
unfinished
unflattering
unfortunate
unfortunately
ungainly
uniform
uniformity
unify
uninsured
union
unionist
unique
unison
unit/e
unity
universal
universe
university

unknowingly
unknown
unless
unleash
unlikely
unload
unlock
unlucky
unnecessary
unofficial
unofficially
unorthodox
unpredictable
unprepared
unproductive
unquestionably
unravel
unrest
unroll
unruffled
unseasonal

unseasonable
unscrupulous
unsure
unsympathetic
untangle
untidy
until
unusual
unusually
unwanted
unwary
unwelcome
unwell
unwieldy
unwilling
unwillingly
unwillingness
unyielding
unzip
up
uphold
upholster
upholstery
upkeep
upon
upper (b)
upper case
upper class
upper hand
uppermost
upper storey
upright
uproar
uproot
upset
upshot
upside-down
upstairs
upstart
upwards
uranium
urban/e
urchin
Urdu
urge
urgency
urgent
urn
us/e
usable
usage
useful
useless
user
usher
usual
usually
usurp
usury
utensil
utility
utilize
utmost

utopia ....

utter ....

utterance ....

utterly ....

vacancy ....

vacant ....

vacate ....

vacation ....

vaccinate ....

vaccination ....

vaccine ....

vacillate ....

vacuous ....

vacuum ....

vagabond ....

vagary ....

vagrant ....

vague ....

vail/vale/veil ....

vain ....

vainly ....

valance ....

valediction ....

valency ....

valentine ....

vales ....

valet ....

valiant ....

valid ....

validate ....

validity ....

valise ....

valley ....

valleys ....

valour ....

valuable ....

valuation
value
valueless
valuer
valve
vamp
vampire
van
vandal
vandalism
vanguard
vanilla or
vanish or
vanity
vanquish
vantage
vaporize
vapour
variable
variance
variant

variegate
varies
variety
various
varnish
vary
vase
vaseline
vast
vat/VAT
vaudeville
vault
vaunt
veal
veer/ed
vegetable
vegetarian
vegetate
vegetation
vehemence or
vehement or

vehicle
vehicular
vein
vellum
velocity
velour
velvet
vending
vendetta
veneer
venerable
venerate
veneration
Venetian
vengeance
vengeful
venison
venom
vent
ventilate
ventilation

ventilator
ventriloquist
venture
venue
Venus
veracious
veranda
verb
verbal
verbatim
verbose
verdant
verdict
verge
verger
verification
verify or
verity or
vermin
versatile
versatility

verse
version
versus
vertical
very
vessel
vest
vestibule
vestige
vestments
vestry
vet
veteran
veterinary
veto
vex
vexation
vexed
via
viable
viaduct

vibrant
vibrate
vibration
vibrator
vicar
vicarage
vicarious
vice
victim
victimization
victimize
victor
victory
victual
victualler
vie
vied
video (b)
view
viewer
vigil

vigilance

vigilant

vigour

vigorous

vile

vilify

villa

village

villain

villainous

vim

vindicate

vindication

vindictive

vine

vinegar

vineyard

vintage

vintner

vinyl or

violate

violation

violence

violent

violet

violin

violinist

viper

virgin

virile

virtual

virtue/s

virtuoso

virtuous

virus

visa

visage or

viscose

viscount

visible

visibility

visibly

vision

visionary

visit

visitation

visitor

visor

vista

visual

visualized

vital

vitality

vitamin

vitreous

vivacious

vivid

vivisection

vixen

vocabulary

vocal

vocalist

vocalize

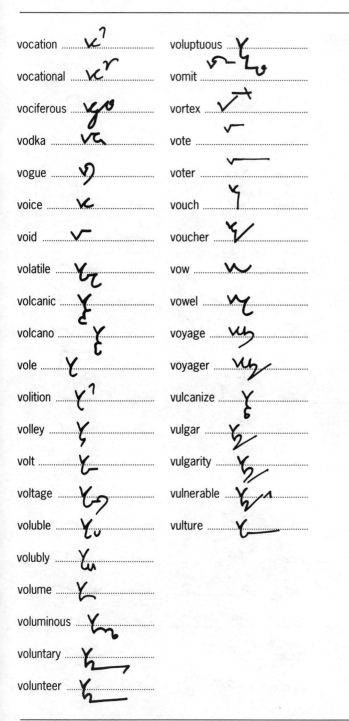

vocation ....

vocational ....

vociferous ....

vodka ....

vogue ....

voice ....

void ....

volatile ....

volcanic ....

volcano ....

vole ....

volition ....

volley ....

volt ....

voltage ....

voluble ....

volubly ....

volume ....

voluminous ....

voluntary ....

volunteer ....

voluptuous ....

vomit ....

vortex ....

vote ....

voter ....

vouch ....

voucher ....

vow ....

vowel ....

voyage ....

voyager ....

vulcanize ....

vulgar ....

vulgarity ....

vulnerable ....

vulture ....

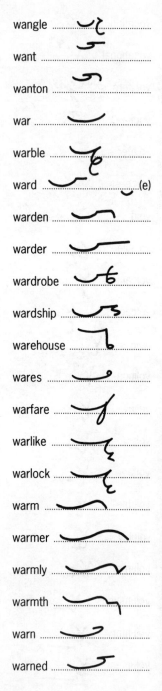

wad/e

waddle

wader

wafer

waffle

waft/ed

wag/e

wager

waggle

wagon

waif

wail

waist

wait

waiter

waive

wake

wakeful

waken

walk

walkabout

walker

wall or

wallaby

wallet

wallop

wallow

walnut

walrus

waltz

wan

wand

wander

wanderer

wangle

want

wanton

war

warble

ward (e)

warden

warder

wardrobe

wardship

warehouse

wares

warfare

warlike

warlock

warm

warmer

warmly

warmth

warn

warned

warp	watery	weary
warrant	watt	weasel
warranty	wattle	weather
warren	wave	weatherman
warrior	waver	weave
warship	wax	weaver
wart	waxen	web
was	waxworks	wedding
wash	way	wedge
washer	wayside	wedlock
washes	wayward	**Wednesday**
wasp	**we**	wee
waste	weak	weed
wasteful	weaker	week
wastefulness	weakness	weekday
wastrel	weal	weekend
watch	wealth/y	weep
watcher	wean	weevil
watchful	weapon	weft
watchfulness	wear	weigh
water	weariness	weighed

weight

weird

welch

welcome

weld

welfare

well

well-being or

well-educated

well-groomed

well-known

well-off

well-planned

wellingtons

Welsh

welt

went

were

west

westerly

western

westward

wet

whale

wharf or

wharves or

what

whatever

wheat

wheedle

wheel

wheeze

whelk

whelp

when

whence

whenever

where

whereas

whereby

wherein

whereupon

wherewithal

whether

which

whichever

whiff

whig

while

whilst

whim

whimper

whine

whip

whippet

whirl

whisk

whisker

whisky

whisper

whist

whistle

whistler

white .... or ....
Whitehall ....
whiting .... or ....
Whitsun .... or ....
whittle ....
who ....
whoever ....
whole ....
wholemeal ....
wholesale ....
wholesaler ....
wholly ....
whom ....
whore ....
whorl ....
whose ....
why ....
wick ....
wicked ....
wicket ....
wide ....(e)

widely ....
widow ....
widower ....
width ....
wield ....
wife ....
wig ....
wiggle ....
wigwam ....
wild ....
wilderness ....
wilful ....
will ....
willing ....
willingly ....
willow ....
wilt ....
Wimbledon .... or ....
wimple ....
win ....
wince ....

winch ....
wind ....
windmill ....
window ....
windy ....
wine ....
wing ....
winner ....
winter ....
wipe ....
wiper ....
wire ....
wireless ....
wisdom ....
wise ....
wish ....
wishful ....
wisp ....
wistful ....
wit ....
witch ....

with
withdraw
withdrawn
wither
within
without
withstand
witness
witnessed
witnesses
witticism
wittingly
witty
wives
wizard
wobble
wobbly
woe
woke
wold
wolf

wolves
woman
womb
wombat
women
won
wonder
wonderful ... or
wonderfully
wondrous
woo
wood
wooden
woof
wool
woollen
word ... (e/g)
word processing
word processor
wore
work

workable
worker
workforce
workman
workmanship
workmen
workshop
world
world-wide
worm
worried
worry
worse
worship
worst
worsted
worth
worthless
would ... (g)
wound
wrack

wraith ....

wrangle ....

wrangler ....

wrap ....

wrapper ....

wrath ....

wreak ....

wreath ....

wreck ....

wreckage ....

wrecker ....

wren ....

wrench ....

wrest ....

wrestle ....

wretch ....

wriggle ....

wright ....

wring ....

wrinkle ....

wrist ....

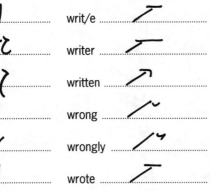

writ/e ....

writer ....

written ....

wrong ....

wrongly ....

wrote ....

X

xenon ....

Xerox ....

Xmas ....

X-ray ....

xylophone ....

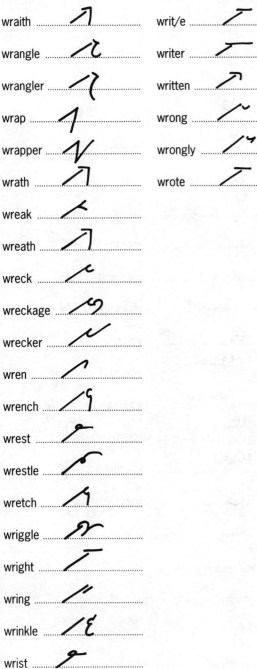

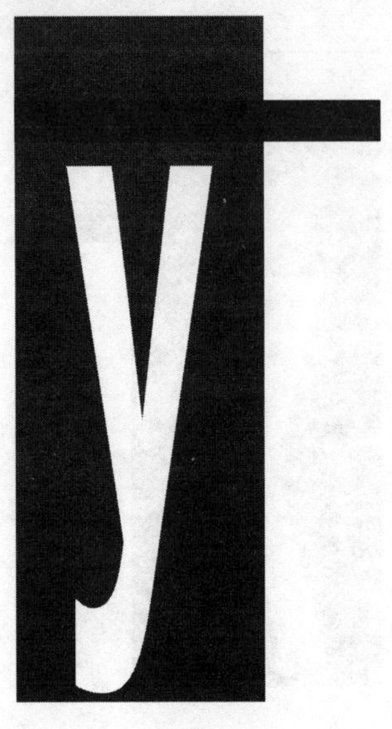

yacht ....

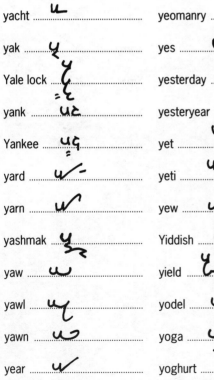

yak ....

Yale lock ....

yank ....

Yankee ....

yard ....

yarn ....

yashmak ....

yaw ....

yawl ....

yawn ....

year ....

yearling ....

yearly ....

yearn ....

yeast ....

yell ....

yellow ....

yelp ....

yen ....

yeoman ....

yeomanry ....

yes ....

yesterday ....

yesteryear ....

yet ....

yeti ....

yew ....

Yiddish ....

yield ....

yodel ....

yoga ....

yoghurt ....

yoke ....

yokel ....

yolk ....

yon ....

yonder ....

you ....

young ....

younger ....

youngest ....

youngster ....

your ....

yourself ....

yourselves ....

youth ....

youthful ....

yowl ....

yule ....

Z

zombie
zone
zoo
zoologist
zoology
zoom
Zulu

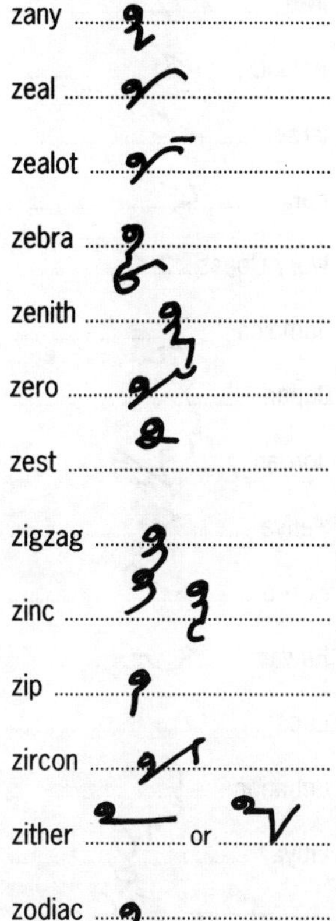
zany
zeal
zealot
zebra
zenith
zero
zest
zigzag
zinc
zip
zircon
zither or
zodiac

Appendix 1
Countries

Afghanistan
Albania
Algeria
Angola
Argentina
Australia
Austria
Bangladesh
Belgium
Bolivia
Brazil
Bulgaria
Burkina Faso
Burma
Cambodia
Cameroon
Canada
Chad
Chile
China
Colombia
Commonwealth of Independent States
Congo ... or ...
Croatia
Cuba
Cyprus
Czechoslovakia
Denmark
Dominican Republic
Ecuador
Egypt
Eire
England
Ethiopia
Finland
France
Germany
Ghana
Great Britain
Greece
Greenland
Guatemala
Guinea
Haiti
Holland
Hong Kong
Hungary
Iceland
India
Indonesia
Iran
Iraq
Ireland
Israel
Italy
Ivory Coast
Jamaica
Japan
Jordan
Kenya
Korea
Kuwait
Laos
Lebanon
Libya
Luxembourg

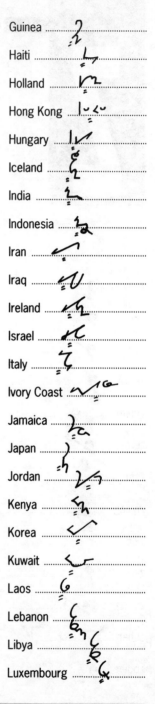

Madagascar ....

Malawi ....

Malaysia ....

Mali ....

Malta ....

Mauritania ....

Mexico ....

Mongolia ....

Morocco ....

Mozambique ....

Nepal ....

Netherlands ....

New Zealand ....

Nicaragua ....

Niger ....

Nigeria ....

Northern Ireland ....

Norway ....

Pakistan ....

Panama ....

Papua New Guinea ....

Paraguay ....

Peru ....

Philippines ....

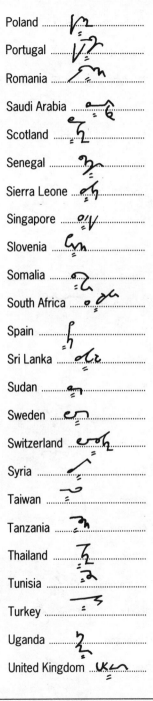

Poland ....

Portugal ....

Romania ....

Saudi Arabia ....

Scotland ....

Senegal ....

Sierra Leone ....

Singapore ....

Slovenia ....

Somalia ....

South Africa ....

Spain ....

Sri Lanka ....

Sudan ....

Sweden ....

Switzerland ....

Syria ....

Taiwan ....

Tanzania ....

Thailand ....

Tunisia ....

Turkey ....

Uganda ....

United Kingdom .....UK.....

United States ....

Uruguay ....

Venezuela ....

Vietnam ....

Wales ....

Yemen ....

Yugoslavia ....

Zaire ....

Zambia ....

Zimbabwe ....

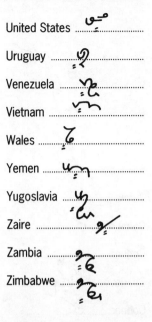

Appendix 2
Towns and cities

Australia

Adelaide ....

Albany ....

Alice Springs ....

Ballarat ....

Barcaldine ....

Bendigo ....

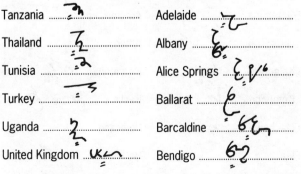

Bourke

Brisbane or

Broken Hill

Broome

Bunbury

Bundabe

Cairns

Canberra

Ceduna

Charleville

Cobnar

Cooktown

Cunnamulla

Darwin

Derby

Esperance

Fremantle

Geelong

Geraldton

Halls Creek

Kalgoorlie

Katherine

Mackay

Maitland

Melbourne

Newcastle

Narrabri

Normanton

Nyngan

Perth

Rockhampton

Surfers Paradise

Sydney

Taree

Townsville

Warwick

Whyalla

Winton

Wollongong

Wyndham

Europe

Alicante

Amsterdam

Athens

Barcelona

Basle or

Belgrade

Berlin

Bergen

Biarritz

Bologna

Bordeaux

Boulogne

Bourges

Bremen

Brest or

Brussels

Bucharest

Budapest

Cadiz

Calais

Cherbourg

Cologne

Copenhagen

Cordoba

Dieppe

Dijon

Dresden

Dubrovnik

Florence

Frankfurt

Geneva

Genoa ....

Gibraltar ....

Granada ....

Grenoble ....

Hamburg ....

Hanover ....

Helsinki ....

Innsbrück ....

Kiel ....

Le Havre ....

Lille ....

Limoges ....

Lisbon ....

Lyons .... or ....

Madrid ....

Malaga ....

Malmö ....

Marseille ....

Messina ....

Milan ....

Monte Carlo ....

Moscow ....

Munich ....

Nantes ....

Naples ....

Narbonne ....

Nice ....

Narvik ....

Nuremberg ....

Oporto ....

Orléans ....

Oslo ....

Palermo ....

Palma ....

Paris ....

Pisa ....

Prague ....

Reims ....

Rennes ....

Rome ....

Roscoff ....

Rotterdam ....

Salzburg ....

St Mâlo ....

San Sebastián ....

Santander ....

Seville ....

Split ....

Stockholm ....

Strasbourg ....

Stuttgart ....

Toulouse ....

Tours ....

Trieste ....

Turin ....

Valencia ....

Venice ....

Vienna ....

Warsaw ....

Zürich ....

New Zealand

Auckland ....

Christchurch ....

Dunedin ....

Hamilton ....

Queenstown ....

Wanganui ....

Wellington ....

North America and Canada

Abilene ....

Albuquerque ....

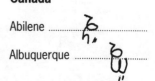

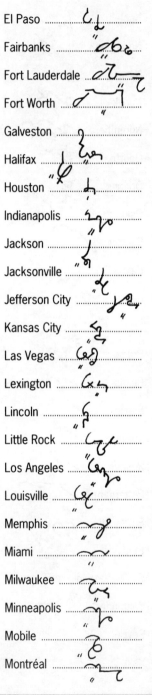

Amarillo	El Paso	Nashville
Anchorage	Fairbanks	New Orleans
Atlanta	Fort Lauderdale	New York
Augusta	Fort Worth	Oakland
Balitmore	Galveston	Oklahoma City
Baton Rouge	Halifax	Omaha
Birmingham	Houston	Orlando
Boston	Indianapolis	Ottowa
Buffalo	Jackson	Philadelphia ... or
Calgary	Jacksonville	Phoenix
Carson City	Jefferson City	Pittsburgh
Charleston	Kansas City	Portland
Chattanooga	Las Vegas	Providence
Chicago	Lexington	Québec
Cincinnati	Lincoln	Richmond ... or
Clarksville	Little Rock	Sacramento ... or
Cleveland	Los Angeles	St Louis
Columbus	Louisville	St Paul
Dallas	Memphis	Salt Lake City
Dayton	Miami	San Antonio
Denver	Milwaukee	San Diego
Detroit	Minneapolis	San Francisco
Duluth	Mobile	San José
Edmonton	Montréal	Savannah

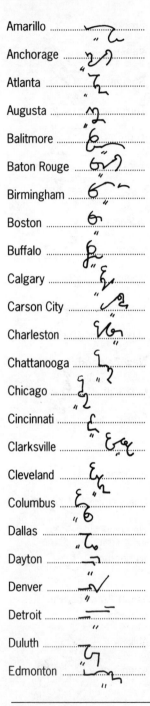

Seattle ....

Springfield ....

Tallahassee ....

Tampa ....

Toledo ....

Topeka ....

Toronto ....

Tucson ....

Tulsa ....

Vancouver ....

Victoria ....

Washington ....

Wichita ....

Winnipeg ....

Central and South America

Acapulco ....

Belém ....

Belize City ....

Belo Horizonte ....

Bogotá .... or ....

Brasilia ....

Buenos Aires ....

Cali ....

Caracas ....

Cartagena ....

Chihuahua ....

Córdoba ....

Durango ....

Fortaleza ....

Georgetown ....

Guadalajara ....

Guatemala ....

Guayaquil ....

La Paz ....

Lima ....

Managua ....

Maracaibo ....

Medellín ....

Mendoza ....

Mérida ....

Mexico City ....

Montería ....

Monterrey ....

Montevideo ....

Panamá ....

Puebla ....

Quito ....

Recife ....

Rio de Janeiro ....

Salvador ....

San Salvador ....

Santa Cruz ....

Santiago ....

Veracruz ....

United Kingdom, Northern Ireland and Eire

Aberdeen ....

Aberystwyth ....

Accrington ....

Aldershot ....

Ayr ....

Banbury ....

Barnsley ....

Barrow-in-Furness ....

Basildon ....

Basingstoke ....

Bath ....

Bedford ....

Belfast ....

Berwick-upon-Tweed ....

Birkenhead
Brimingham
Blackburn
Blackpool
Bolton
Boston
Bournemouth
Bradford
Bridgend
Bridlington
Brighton or
Bristol
Bude
Burnley
Bury
Buxton
Cambridge
Canterbury
Cardiff
Carlisle
Chelmsford
Cheltenham
Chester
Chesterfield

Chichester
Colwyn Bay
Cork
Coventry
Cromer
Croydon or
Darlington
Derby
Dornoch
Douglas
Dover
Dublin
Dundee
Dunstable
Durham
Eastbourne
Edinburgh
Epsom
Exeter
Fareham
Farnborough
Felixstowe
Fife
Fishguard

Folkestone
Gairloch
Galloway
Galway
Gateshead
Glasgow
Glastonbury
Gloucester
Great Yarmouth
Grimsby
Guildford
Harlow
Harrogate
Harrow
Hastings
Hemel Hempstead
Hereford
Hertford
Holyhead
Horsham
Hounslow
Hove
Huddersfield

Hull ....

Ilford ....

Ilfracombe ....

Inverness ....

Ipswich ....

Jarrow ....

Kendal ....

Kettering ....

Kidderminster ....

King's Lynn ....

Kingston-upon-Thames ....

Lancaster ....

Leatherhead ....

Leeds ....

Leicester ....

Lichfield ....

Limerick ....

Lincoln ....

Liverpool ....

Llandudno ....

London ....

Londonderry ....

Lowestoft ....

Luton ....

Maidenhead ....

Maidstone ....

Manchester ....

Margate ....

Middlesbrough ....

Milton Keynes ....

Monmouth ....

Morecambe ....

Motherwell ....

Newbury ....

Newcastle-upon-Tyne ....

Newhaven ....

Newport ....

Newquay ....

Northampton ....

Norwich ....

Nottingham ....

Oban ....

Oldham ....

Oxford ....

Paisley ....

Perth ....

Peterborough ....

Peterlee ....

Plymouth ....

Porthcawl ....

Portsmouth ....

Port Talbot ....

Preston ....

Pwllheli ....

Ramsgate ....

Reading ....

Redcar ....

Reigate ....

Rhyl ....

Richmond ....

Ripon ....

Romford ....

Rugby ....

Salford ....

Salisbury ....

Scarborough ....

Sevenoaks ....

Sheffield ....

Shrewsbury ....

Skegness ....

Slough
Southampton
Southend
South Shields
Stafford
Stamford
Stevenage
Stirling
Stockport
Stoke-on-Trent
Stonehaven
Stranraer
Sunderland
Swansea
Swindon
Taunton
Tenby
Thurso
Tiverton
Torbay
Torquay
Truro
Ventnor
Wakefield
Walsall
Warrington
Watford
Welwyn
Wembley
West Bromwich
Weston-super-Mare
Weymouth
Whitby
Wick
Wimbourne
Winchester
Windsor
Woking
Wolverhampton
Worcester
Worthing
Yarmouth
York

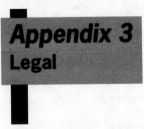

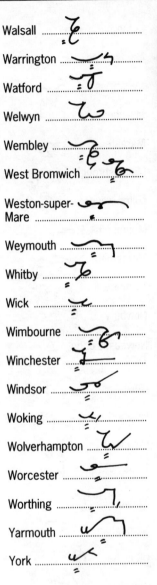

Appendix 3
Legal

Words in bold type indicate a reduced or special outline; words followed by (*Lat*) indicate Latin terminology.

abatement
abduction
absconding
absolute
abuttals
ACAS
acceptor
access
accident
accretion
accused
acquittal
action
Act
Act of Parliament
actuary
adaptation

ademption
ad hoc (*Lat*)
administrator
admission
adultery
ad valorem (*Lat*)
advocate
advowson
affidavit
affiliate
affirmation or
affray
agency
agent
airside
alias
alibi
aliter (*Lat*)
aliunde (*Lat*)
allocatur (*Lat*)
allonge (*Lat*)
amendment
annuitant
annuity

answer
ante (*Lat*)
anticipation
appeal
appellant
appraisement
appropriation
arbitrage
arbitration
arbitrator
arraignment
arrest or
arson or
articles
assault
Assizes
assured
assurer
attest
attestation
audit
authority
automatism
bail

bailee
bailiff
bailment
bailor
bankrupt
Bar
baratry
barrister
barter
battery
bear
bearer
belligerent
Bencher
beneficiary
bequest
bicameralism
bigamy
billeting
blackmail
bona fides (*Lat*)
bona vacantia (*Lat*)
bond
boundary or

bribe ....
brief .... or ....
brokerage ....
budget ....
bull ....
burglary ....
bye-laws ....
Cabinet ....
capacity ....
cartel ....
caveat (*Lat*) ....
caveato (*Lat*) ....
certioari (*Lat*) ....
cession ....
chambers ....
champerty ....
Chancery ....
charge .... or ....
charterparty ....
chattels ....
cheque ....
circuit ....
citation ....
civil ....

closure ....
codicil .... or ....
codified ....
coercion ....
cognating ....
collusion ....
Comecon ....
commissioner ....
commorientes (*Lat*) ....
commutation ....
compellability ....
compensation ....
competency ....
completion ....
compulsory ....
concealment ....
condemnation ....
condition ....
conditional ....
condonation ....
conference ....
confession ....
confusio (*Lat*) ....
conjugal ....

connivance ....
conquest ....
consensu (*Lat*) ....
consent ....
consideration ....
consignor ....
consolidation ....
consortium ....
conspiracy ....
constable ....
constitutional ....
constructive ....
consular ....
consultation ....
contango (*Lat*) ....
contra (*Lat*) ....
contraband ....
contract ....
contributory ....
convention ....
conversion ....
conveyance ....
conviction ....
copyright ....

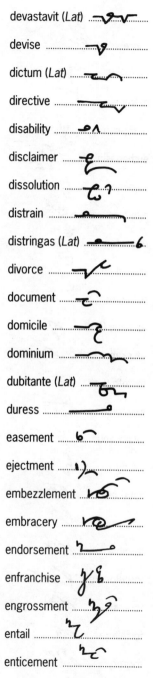

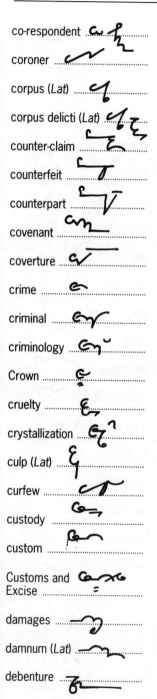

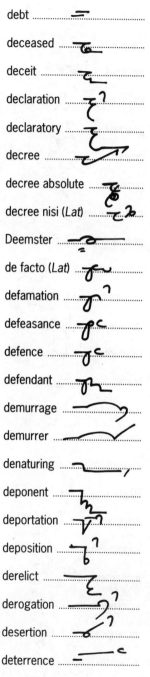

co-respondent
coroner
corpus (*Lat*)
corpus delicti (*Lat*)
counter-claim
counterfeit
counterpart
covenant
coverture
crime
criminal
criminology
Crown
cruelty
crystallization
culp (*Lat*)
curfew
custody
custom
Customs and Excise
damages
damnum (*Lat*)
debenture

debt
deceased
deceit
declaration
declaratory
decree
decree absolute
decree nisi (*Lat*)
Deemster
de facto (*Lat*)
defamation
defeasance
defence
defendant
demurrage
demurrer
denaturing
deponent
deportation
deposition
derelict
derogation
desertion
deterrence

devastavit (*Lat*)
devise
dictum (*Lat*)
directive
disability
disclaimer
dissolution
distrain
distringas (*Lat*)
divorce
document
domicile
dominium
dubitante (*Lat*)
duress
easement
ejectment
embezzlement
embracery
endorsement
enfranchise
engrossment
entail
enticement

equity
escrow
estoppel
estreat
European
euthanasia
evidence
examiner
executed
execution
executor
ex facie (*Lat*)
ex gratia (*Lat*)
ex toto (*Lat*)
extradition
falsification
felony
fiat (*Lat*)
flotation
forcible
foreclosure
forensic
forfeiture
forgery

fraud
fraudulent
freehold
gazumping
goodwill
grantee
guarantee
guarantor
guillotine
habendum (*Lat*)
habeas corpus (*Lat*)
Hansard
headnote
homicide
hotchpot
ibid (*Lat*)
idem (*Lat*)
illegal
illegitimacy
impeachment
incitement
incorporation
incumbrance
in delicto (*Lat*)

indemnity
indentures
indicia (*Lat*)
indictment
infanticide
infra (*Lat*)
infringement
injunction
innuendo
inquest
interlocutory
intestacy
intimidation
in toto (*Lat*)
ipso facto (*Lat*)
jobber
judgement
judicial
judiciary
jurisprudence
juror
jury
jus (*Lat*)
justice or

juvenile ....
kleptomania ....
laches ....
larceny ....
law ....
lawyer ....
leasehold ....
legacy ....
legal ....
legatee ....
legislation ....
legislature ....
legitimacy ....
levy ....
liability ....
libel ....
licence ....
lien ....
liquidator ....
litigation ....
magistrate ....
maintenance ....
malice ....
malicious ....

malversion ....
mandate ....
manifest ....
manslaughter ....
matrimony ....
matrimonial ....
maturity ....
messuage ....
minor ....
misdemeanour ....
misfeasance ....
misrepresentation ....
mitigation ....
moiety ....
monogamy ....
moratorium (*Lat*) ....
mortgage ....
multinational ....
muniments ....
murder ....
naturalization ....
negligent ....
negligence ....
negotiability ....

nexus (*Lat*) ....
nominee ....
non compus mentis (*Lat*) ....
non constat (*Lat*) ....
novation ....
nuisance ....
nullity ....
oath ....
obligor ....
obviousness ....
offeree ....
offeror ....
pardon ....
parole ....
partition ....
partnership ....
passim (*Lat*) ....
patent ....
patrial ....
pawn ....
pawnbroker ....
penology ....
per (*Lat*) ....

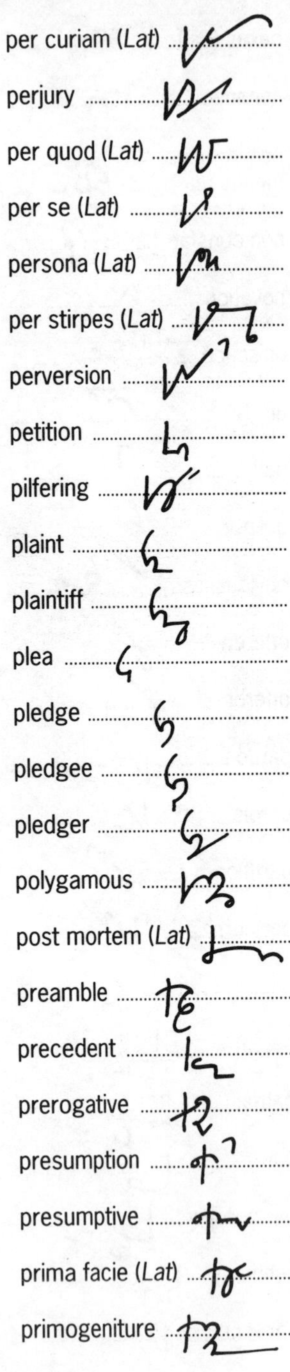

per curiam (*Lat*)
perjury
per quod (*Lat*)
per se (*Lat*)
persona (*Lat*)
per stirpes (*Lat*)
perversion
petition
pilfering
plaint
plaintiff
plea
pledge
pledgee
pledger
polygamous
post mortem (*Lat*)
preamble
precedent
prerogative
presumption
presumptive
prima facie (*Lat*)
primogeniture

prisoner
probate
probation
Procurator Fiscal
prohibition
promissory
provocation
proxy
pupillage
qua (*Lat*)
quaere (*Lat*)
quantum (*Lat*)
quantum valebant (*Lat*)
quasi (*Lat*)
quid pro quo (*Lat*)
quondam (*Lat*)
quorum (*Lat*)
realty
receiver
recorder
rectification
reddendum (*Lat*)
registered
Registrar

Regulations
remand
remission
renunciation
reprieve
rescission
res gastae (*Lat*)
residual
residue
res integra (*Lat*)
res judicata (*Lat*)
res nullius (*Lat*)
respondent
restitution
restraint
res vendita (*Lat*)
retainer
reversion
reversioner
revocation
robbery
rout
rummage
salvage

secus (*Lat*) ....
sedition ....
sed quare (*Lat*) ....
seizure ....
sequestration ....
severability ....
sic (*Lat*) ....
slander ....
Solicitor General ....
stare decisis (*Lat*) ....
status quo (*Lat*) ....
statute ....
stet (*Lat*) ....
subject to contract ....
subpoena ....
subrogation ....
subsidiary ....
sub titulo (*Lat*) ....
succession ....
summons ....
surety ....
survivorship ....
syndicate ....
take-over ....

tariff ....
tenancy ....
testator (*Lat*) ....
testatrix (*Lat*) ....
testatum (*Lat*) ....
testimonium ....
title ....
tort ....
traverse ....
treason ....
Treasury ....
trespass ....
trustee ....
unlawful ....
unsecured ....
usufruct ....
verbatim (*Lat*) ....
verdict ....
vice-versa (*Lat*) ....
vis major (*Lat*) ....
viz. (*Lat*) ....
waiver ....
ward of court ....
warrant ....

warranty ....
widow ....
widower ....
winding-up ....
witness ....
witnesses ....
writ ....
yield ....

Appendix 4
Medical words

abdomen ....
abdominal ....
abnormal ....
abnormality ....
abortion ....
abrasion ....
abscess ....
acephalous ....
achalasia ....
acid fast bacilli ....

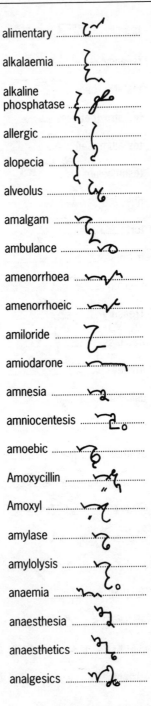

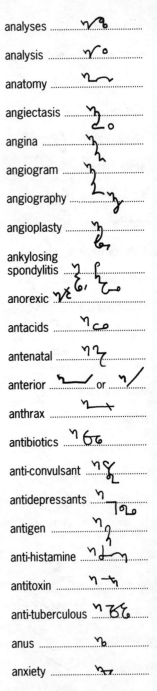

acidaemia
acidity
acidosis
acidotic
acneform
acromegaly
actinic keratosis
acuities
acute
adducted
adenectomy
adenoid
adenoidectomy
adenoma
adenopathy
adhesions
adipose
adnexae
adrenalin
aerophagia
afebrile
afterbirth
AIDS
algesia
alimentary
alkalaemia
alkaline phosphatase
allergic
alopecia
alveolus
amalgam
ambulance
amenorrhoea
amenorrhoeic
amiloride
amiodarone
amnesia
amniocentesis
amoebic
Amoxycillin
Amoxyl
amylase
amylolysis
anaemia
anaesthesia
anaesthetics
analgesics
analyses
analysis
anatomy
angiectasis
angina
angiogram
angiography
angioplasty
ankylosing spondylitis
anorexic
antacids
antenatal
anterior or
anthrax
antibiotics
anti-convulsant
antidepressants
antigen
anti-histamine
antitoxin
anti-tuberculous
anus
anxiety

aorta
apathy ... or ...
apex
aphasia ... or ...
apical
apnoea
appendicitis
appendix
apyrexial
areola
arrhythmia ... or ...
arterial
arteriography
arteritis
artery
arthralgia
arthritic
arthritis
astigmatism
asymptomatic
ataxia
Atenolol
atheroma ... or ...
atrial

atrophic ... or ...
atypical
auditory
aural
aureola
auricle
auscultation
autism
autistic
autopsy
axillary
axis
bacteria
bacterium
barium ... or ...
barium enema ... or ...
barium meal ... or ...
barium swallow
basal
basophilia
benign
bicornulate
bilateral ... or ...
bilaterally ... or ...

biliary tract disease
bilirubin
biochemistry
biopsy
bladder
bleeding piles
blenorrhagia
blockage
blood count
blood pressure ... or ...
blood sugar ... or ...
blood tests
blood transfusion
botulism
bowel
brachial
bradycardia
breathlessness
breech
bromide
bronchi ... or ...
bronchitis ... or ...
bronchophony ... or ...

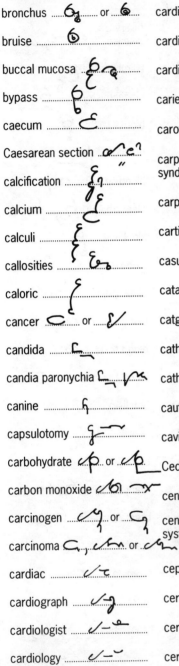

bronchus .... or ....

bruise ....

buccal mucosa ....

bypass ....

caecum ....

Caesarean section ....

calcification ....

calcium ....

calculi ....

callosities ....

caloric ....

cancer .... or ....

candida ....

candia paronychia ....

canine ....

capsulotomy ....

carbohydrate .... or ....

carbon monoxide ....

carcinogen .... or ....

carcinoma .... or ....

cardiac ....

cardiograph ....

cardiologist ....

cardiology ....

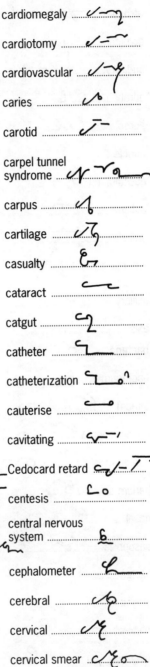

cardiomegaly ....

cardiotomy ....

cardiovascular ....

caries ....

carotid ....

carpel tunnel syndrome ....

carpus ....

cartilage ....

casualty ....

cataract ....

catgut ....

catheter ....

catheterization ....

cauterise ....

cavitating ....

Cedocard retard ....

centesis ....

central nervous system ....

cephalometer ....

cerebral ....

cervical ....

cervical smear ....

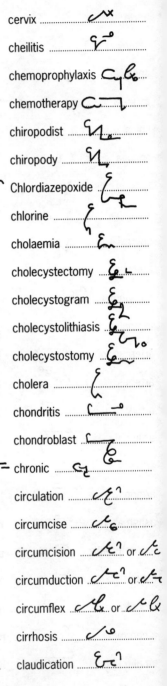

cervix ....

cheilitis ....

chemoprophylaxis ....

chemotherapy ....

chiropodist ....

chiropody ....

Chlordiazepoxide ....

chlorine ....

cholaemia ....

cholecystectomy ....

cholecystogram ....

cholecystolithiasis ....

cholecystostomy ....

cholera ....

chondritis ....

chondroblast ....

chronic ....

circulation ....

circumcise ....

circumcision .... or ....

circumduction .... or ....

circumflex .... or ....

cirrhosis ....

claudication ....

cleft palate

clinical

clinically

clotting time ... or ...

coalescing

coccyx

colectomy

colicky

colitis

colonic

colpitis

coma

concussion

confinement ... or ...

congenital

congestive cardiac failure

conjunctivitis ... or ...

consciousness

constipation

contraception

contraceptive

contractions

contractures

contra-indicated

convalescence

convulsions

cornea

coronary

corpus

cortex

costal

cramp

craniectomy

cranium

crepitation

cretin

critical

croup

cruciate ligaments

cryogenic

cryopexy

culture

curettage

cusp

cyanosed

cyanosis

cyst

cystalgia

cystectomy

cystic fibrosis ... or ...

cystitis

cystogram

cystoscopy

cytology

dandruff ... or ...

debilitate

debility ... or ...

decorticated

defecation ... or ...

dehydrated

dehydration

dentalgia

depression

dermatitis

dermatology

dermis

detoxification

dexterity

dextrose

diabetes

diabetes mellitus

diabetic
diagnoses
diagnosis ... or ... or △
dialysis
diaphragm
diarrhoea
diastolic
dietetic
digestive
digoxin
dilatation
dilate
dilation
diplegia
discharge summary
dislocated
distal
distension
diuretics
dizziness ... or
dorsal
dorsiflexion
dorsum
dosage
douche
duct
duodenal ulcer
dysaesthesia
dysentery
dysgenesis
dyslexia
dyslexic
dysmenorrhoea
dyspepsia
dysphagia
dysplasia
dyspnoea
dysraphism
dystrophy ... or
earache
ectoderm
ectopic
ectopic pregnancy
eczema
effusions ... or
electrocardiogram ... or
electroconvulsive
therapy ... or
electro-encephalogram
electrolytes
electrotherapy
elixir
emaciated
embolism
encapsulation
encephalitis
encopresis
endocrine
endometrium
enema
enteralgia
enteritis
enuresis
enzyme
epicardium
epidemic
epidermis
epidural
epigastric
epigastrium

epiglottis
epilepsy
epileptic
episode
equinus
erythema
erythromycin
ethambutol
eversion ... or ...
exacerbate ... or ...
exacerbations ... or ...
excision
excretion
exophoria ... or ...
exophthalmic ... or ...
expectorant
expiratory
extensor
faecal
faeces
Fallopian tube
femora
femoral
femur

fertilization
fertility ... or ...
fever
fibrilla ... or ...
fibrillation ... or ...
fibro-adenoma ... or ...
fibrocystic ... or ...
fibrocyte ... or ...
fibroids
fibroma
fibrous
fibula ... or ...
fissure ... or ...
fistula
flatulence
foci ... or ...
foetus
follicle
follicular
formalin ... or ...
fornix
fracture
frontal
frusemide

fundi ... or ...
fundus ... or ...
fungal
fusion
gait
gallstones
ganglion
gangrene
gastroenterologist
gastroscopy ... or ...
general anaesthetic
general surgeon
geneticists
geriatric
gestation
gingivitis
gingivostomatitis
glands
glaucoma
globus hystericus
glossal
glucose
glycogen
grand mal

groin ... or ...
gynaecologist
gynaecology
haematemesis
haemoglobin
haemoptysis
haemorrhage
haemorrhoids
haemostasis
hepatitis
hernia
herniotomies
herpetic
hilum
histamine
histological
histology
homosexual
hormonal
humerus
hydrated
hydrocele
hydrosalpinges
hydrosalpinx

hydrotubation
hyperacidity
hyperactive
hyperplasia
hyper-reflexia
hypertension
hypertensive
hypnotics
hypochondriac
hypochondrial
hypochondrium
hypodermic
hypolarynx
hypoplasia
hypotension
hypothermia
hypothyroidism
hysterectomy
hysterosalping-ogram
idiopathic
ileectomy
ileum
iliac crests ... or ...

iliac fossa
iliac region
ilium
illegitimate
illness
immiscible
immune
immunoglobulin
immunologically
impetigo
implant
incision
incisors
incontinent
incubation
indigestion
infarct ... or ...
infarction ... or ...
infection ... or ...
infero-posterior
infertility ... or ...
inflammation ... or ...
infusion ... or ...
inguinal ... or ...

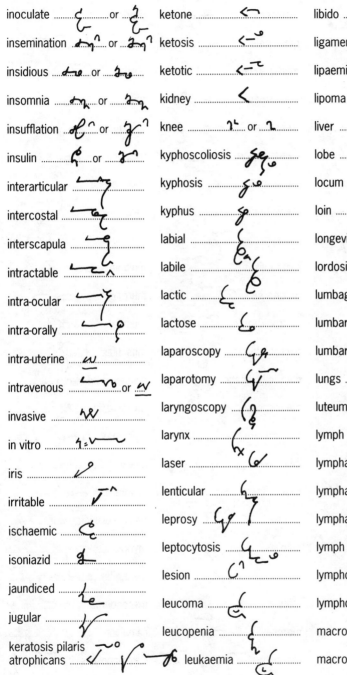

inoculate .... or ....
insemination .... or ....
insidious .... or ....
insomnia .... or ....
insufflation .... or ....
insulin .... or ....
interarticular ....
intercostal ....
interscapula ....
intractable ....
intra-ocular ....
intra-orally ....
intra-uterine ....
intravenous .... or ....
invasive ....
in vitro ....
iris ....
irritable ....
ischaemic ....
isoniazid ....
jaundiced ....
jugular ....
keratosis pilaris atrophicans ....

ketone ....
ketosis ....
ketotic ....
kidney ....
knee .... or ....
kyphoscoliosis ....
kyphosis ....
kyphus ....
labial ....
labile ....
lactic ....
lactose ....
laparoscopy ....
laparotomy ....
laryngoscopy ....
larynx ....
laser ....
lenticular ....
leprosy ....
leptocytosis ....
lesion ....
leucoma ....
leucopenia ....
leukaemia ....

libido ....
ligament ....
lipaemia ....
lipoma ....
liver ....
lobe ....
locum ....
loin ....
longevity ....
lordosis ....
lumbago ....
lumbar ....
lumbar puncture ....
lungs ....
luteum ....
lymph ....
lymphadenectomy ....
lymphadenopathy ....
lymphatic ....
lymph nodes ....
lymphocytosis ....
lymphoma ....
macrocephalous ....
macrocytic ....

macrocytosis
malabsorption
malacia
malaise
malaria
malignancy
malignant
mammary
mammogram
mammography
mandible
mastalgia
mastectomy
mastication
mastoid
maternity
measles
meconium ileus
medication
medicochirurgical
melaena
melanoma
membrane
Menières

meningioma
meningitis
menopausal
menorrhagia
menstrual
menstruation
mesarteritis
mesio-buccal
metabolic
metabolism
metatarsals
metronidazole
microbiology
microcalcification
microscopy
micturition
migraine ... or
miscarriage ... or
mitral
mobility ... or
mongol
morbid
morphine
mortality ... or

mortice
mortuary
motility ... or
mucosa
mucous
mucus
multicellular
multigravida
multipara
multiple sclerosis
murmur
muscle
muscular
myalgia
myasthenia
mycology
myelin
myocardial
myocardial infarction
myopia
myringitis
myxoedema
naevi
narco-analysis

nasal
naso-gastric
nausea
neoplasma or
nephralgia
nephrectomy
nephritis
nephrotomy
nervous system
neuralgia
neurological
neurologist
neuroma
neurotic
neurovascular
nitrogen
nocte
nocturnal
nodes
nodularity
nodules
normoblast
nostril
nulliparous

nutrition
nyctalgia
nystagmus
obstetrics
occlusion
ocular
oculist
oculomotor
odontalgia
odontitis
oedema
oesophagus
oestrogen
omentectomy
omphalitis
omphalocele
onychia
oocyte
oophorectomy
opaque
ophthalmic
ophthalmology
ophthalmoscopy
optic disc

optician
oral
orchidectomy
orchidopexy
orchitis
organic pathology
orthodontic
orthopaedic
orthophoria
orthopnoea
orthoptist
os calcis
osmosis
ossification
osteitis
osteogenic
osteogenesis imperfecta congenita
otalgia
ova
ovarian cyst
ovaries
ovariolysis
ovary

overdose
overhydration
ovulate
ovum
paediatrician
paediatrics
palpable
palpation
palpitation
palsy
panarthritis
pancreas
pancreatic
pancreatitis
paracetamol
paraesthesia
parasitic
paresis .... or
parotid
paroxysmal
parturition
patella
pathological
pathology

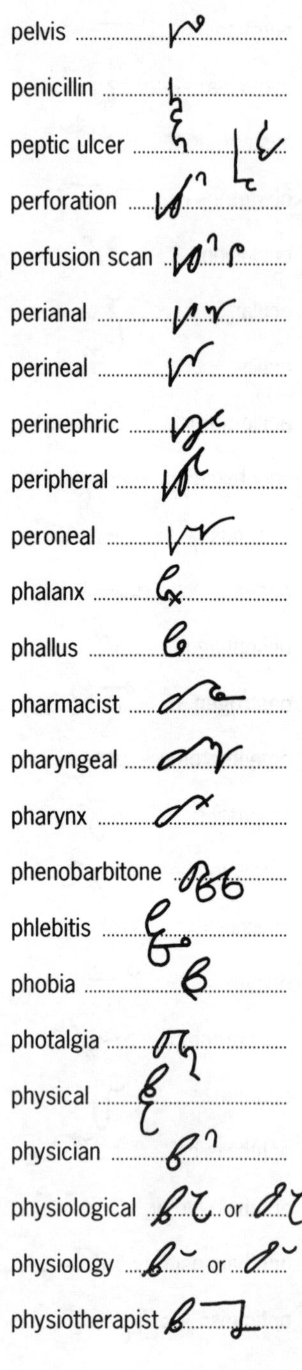

pelvis
penicillin
peptic ulcer
perforation
perfusion scan
perianal
perineal
perinephric
peripheral
peroneal
phalanx
phallus
pharmacist
pharyngeal
pharynx
phenobarbitone
phlebitis
phobia
photalgia
physical
physician
physiological .... or
physiology .... or
physiotherapist

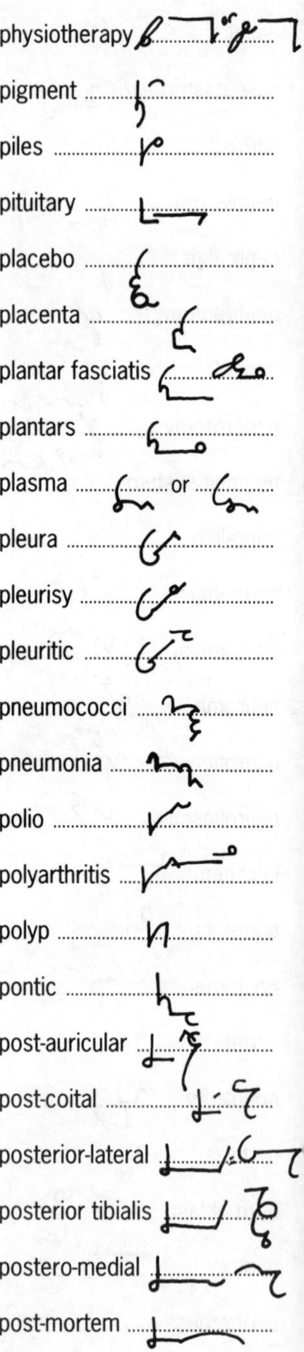

physiotherapy
pigment
piles
pituitary
placebo
placenta
plantar fasciatis
plantars
plasma .... or
pleura
pleurisy
pleuritic
pneumococci
pneumonia
polio
polyarthritis
polyp
pontic
post-auricular
post-coital
posterior-lateral
posterior tibialis
postero-medial
post-mortem

post-natal ....
post-operative ....
practitioner ....
pregnancy ....
premature ....
presbycusis ....
prescription .... or ....
primary ....
prima gravida ....
proctalgia ....
prodromal ....
prognosis .... or ....
Progynova ....
prolapse ....
propranolol ....
proptosis ....
prostate ....
prostatic ....
prosthesis ....
protrusion ....
proximal ....
psoriasis ....
psychiatric ....
psychiatrist ....
psychiatry ....
psychological ....
psychologist ....
psychology ....
psychosis ....
psychosomatic ....
psychotic ....
psychotropics ....
pulmonary ....
pulmonary emboli ....
pulse rate ....
purpura ....
purulent ....
pyaemia ....
pyelitis ....
pyelogram ....
pyelolithotomy ....
pyelonephritis ....
pyrexia ....
quadrant ....
quinsy ....
radiographer ....
radiography ....
radiological ....
radiologist ....
radiology ....
radiotherapy ....
radium ....
rectal ....
rectum ....
referral ....
refract ....
regurgitation ....
renal ....
resection ....
respiration ....
respiratory ....
resuscitate ....
retina ....
retinal ....
rheumatic ....
rheumatoid ....
rheumatology ....
rhinitis ....
rhinology ....
rhinoscopy ....
rhonchi ....
rubella ....

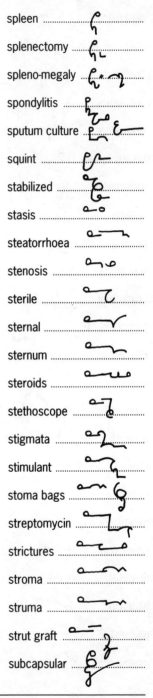

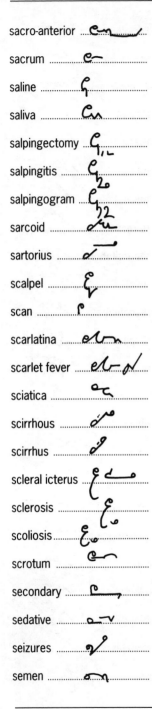

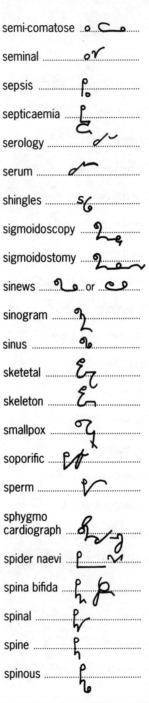

sacro-anterior ....

sacrum ....

saline ....

saliva ....

salpingectomy ....

salpingitis ....

salpingogram ....

sarcoid ....

sartorius ....

scalpel ....

scan ....

scarlatina ....

scarlet fever ....

sciatica ....

scirrhous ....

scirrhus ....

scleral icterus ....

sclerosis ....

scoliosis ....

scrotum ....

secondary ....

sedative ....

seizures ....

semen ....

semi-comatose ....

seminal ....

sepsis ....

septicaemia ....

serology ....

serum ....

shingles ....

sigmoidoscopy ....

sigmoidostomy ....

sinews .... or ....

sinogram ....

sinus ....

sketetal ....

skeleton ....

smallpox ....

soporific ....

sperm ....

sphygmo cardiograph ....

spider naevi ....

spina bifida ....

spinal ....

spine ....

spinous ....

spleen ....

splenectomy ....

spleno-megaly ....

spondylitis ....

sputum culture ....

squint ....

stabilized ....

stasis ....

steatorrhoea ....

stenosis ....

sterile ....

sternal ....

sternum ....

steroids ....

stethoscope ....

stigmata ....

stimulant ....

stoma bags ....

streptomycin ....

strictures ....

stroma ....

struma ....

strut graft ....

subcapsular ....

subchondral ....
sublingual ....
sub talar ....
suicidal ....
supercilium ....
supra-spinatous ....
supra-ventricular ....
suturing ....
swab ....
sycosis ....
symptomatic ....
syndactyl ....
syndrome ....
synovial ....
syphilis ....
syringe ....
systole ....
systolic ....
tachycardia ....
talipes ....
talus ....
tarsal ....
tarsalgia ....
temazepam ....

tendo achilles ....
tendon ....
tendonitis ....
terminal ....
testes ....
testicle ....
testis ....
tetanus ....
tetracoccus ....
therapeutic ....
therapy ....
thermolysis ....
thiamine ....
thoracic ....
thoraco-lumbar ....
thoracoscopy ....
thoracotomy ....
thrombosis ....
thrombotomy ....
thrombus ....
thymectomy ....
thyroid ....
thyrotoxicosis ....
thyroxin ....

tibia ....
tincture ....
tinnitus ....
tocainide ....
tonsillectomy .... or ....
tonsils .... or ....
topical ....
tourniquet ....
toxaemia ....
tracheotomy ....
tranquillizers ....
transection ....
transfusion ....
transplant ....
trauma ....
triceps ....
trichiasis ....
trophic .... or ....
trypsin ....
tubal ....
tuberculosis ....
tuberculous ....
tuberosity ....
tubule ....

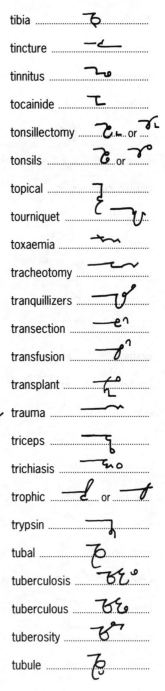

tumour ....
turgid ....
tympanic ....
typhoid ....
ulcers ....
ulnar ....
ultrasound ....
umbilical ....
umbilicus ....
urea .... or ....
uresis ....
ureter ....
urethra ....
urethrocystoscopy ....
uric .... or ....
uric acid ....
urinalysis ....
urinary ....
urine .... or ....
urobilinogen ....
urticaria ....
uterine ....
uterus .... or ....
vaccinate ....

vaccination ....
vaccine ....
vagina ....
valve ....
valvular ....
varicose veins .... or
variococele ....
varus ....
vascular ....
vasectomy ....
vasodilators ....
veins ....
venereal ....
ventilation ....
ventricle ....
ventricular ....
ventriculograph ....
vermicide ....
verruca ....
verrucose ....
vertebrae ....
vertebral ....
vertex ....
vertigo ....

vesicular ....
vessel ....
villi ....
viral hepatitis ....
virology ....
virus ....
vomiting ....
vulva ....
vulvectomy ....
wolfe graft ....
womb ....
wormian ....
xeroderma ....